Border Talk

Border Talk

Writing and Knowing in the Two-Year College

Howard B. Tinberg
Bristol Community College

National Council of Teachers of English
1111 W. Kenyon Road, Urbana, Illinois 61801-1096

Manuscript Editor: Lee Erwin

Production Editor: Michelle Sanden Johlas

Interior Design: Tom Kovacs for TGK Design

Cover Design: Jenny Jensen Greenleaf

NCTE Stock Number 03782-3050

It is the policy of NCTE in its journals and other publications to provide a forum for the open discussion of ideas concerning the content and the teaching of English and the language arts. Publicity accorded to any particular point of view does not imply endorsement by the Executive Committee, the Board of Directors, or the membership at large, except in announcements of policy, where such endorsement is clearly specified.

Library of Congress Cataloging-in-Publication Data

Tinberg, Howard B., 1953–
    Border talk : writing and knowing in the two-year college / Howard B. Tinberg.
       p.   cm.
    Includes bibliographical references (p.) and index.
    ISBN 0-8141-0378-2 (pbk.)
    1. Community college teachers—United States. 2. Community colleges—Unites States. 3. College teaching—United States. 4. English language—Rhetoric—Study and teaching—United States. 5. Language arts—Correlation with content subjects—United States.   I. National Council of Teachers of English. II. Title.
LB2331.72.T56   1997
378.1'25—dc21   97-3901

Contents

Acknowledgments

For three weeks in July of 1994, my colleagues Peter Griffin, Jerry LePage, Kathleen Lund, Carol Martin, Patricia Massey, Marlene Pollock, and Diane Silveria and I engaged in a conversation about writing, reading, knowing, and, of course, teaching, in the disciplines. I want to thank them from the start for engaging in a frank and thoughtful discussion of the things that matter so much to all of us.

I would like to thank as well two men whose efforts in authoring our Title 3 grant set up both our college's writing lab and the annual summer workshops: Paul Fletcher and Ray Lavertue. Quite literally, without these "founding fathers" we would not have been sitting in room D209 for those three weeks.

Also due thanks is Chris Gilbert, our team's learning specialist, who, although unable to attend all our workshop sessions, added immeasurably to the quality and depth of our discussions.

I want to express thanks as well to Greg Cupples, whose technical and office support were invaluable to the smooth running both of the workshop and of the lab generally.

Thanks need to be extended to the peer tutors who attended our workshop—Debra Cupples and Robert Correira—and who contributed an important perspective to our deliberations.

I would also like to acknowledge the ongoing support of our college's administration, especially our president, Eileen Farley, and our dean of academic affairs, David Feeney.

And I want to thank my colleague and friend Ronald Weisberger for offering kind and sage advice on this manuscript.

Last, and most deeply, I want to thank my family and to say, simply, this is for Toni, Miriam, and Leah.

Introduction: Community College Teachers as Border Crossers

Crossing the border evokes ambivalent images. . . .

—Ruth Behar

To teach at a community college is to be "in translation" or between places. With their mission to provide vocational training and to prepare students for transfer to colleges and universities, community colleges have always had a complex purpose (Cohen and Brawer 1982). That complexity colors instruction at all times. What we teach and how we teach must reflect the diverse needs of our students, the needs of those who plan to transfer to four-year institutions and the needs of those who intend to enter the workplace immediately upon graduating from the community college; the needs of traditionally aged students and the needs of so-called returning students, who have spent years out of school. A poem, for example, must be read and taught to suit the complexities of the community college classroom. How will their histories shade students' readings?

The task of tailoring instruction to students' histories and needs has become even more complex as students' numbers increase. The expansion of community college enrollment since the 1960s has been well documented. As of 1988, when the Commission on the Future of Community Colleges published *Building Communities,* nearly half of all undergraduates in the United States attended community colleges (*Building* 1988).

It is hardly surprising, given the range and complexity of our task, that community college faculty are perceived as overworked. But what usually follows is an assumption that community college faculty are teaching drones, burned-out husks of what we once were, with little time and inclination to stay up-to-date on current scholarship and research. In one recent study, two researchers of the community college scene declared that community colleges were everywhere experiencing an "academic crisis," their faculty facing the prospects of little promotion and doomed to teach the same courses year after year (McGrath and Spear 1991). Two-year college faculty, they assert, simply have little opportunity to engage in dialogue with colleagues even down the corridor, let alone in other institutions. They spend more and more class time teaching basic or remedial skills, not the college-level courses that they thought they would be teaching when they began. That picture would seem to be supported by a profile done of a single community college during the 1970s, in which faculty member after faculty member testified to the hindrances to teaching (London 1978). "Sometimes they make life a little difficult," says a math teacher of her students:

> and they come in not having read the chapter that was assigned for the week, not even having tried the home work. Then I usually just go back, give a brief lecture, and then we talk our way through the chapter. Sometimes most of them come in unprepared. (117)

While they describe real problems facing community college teachers, such studies yield very little information about the reflection that accompanies the teaching that two-year college faculty do. We rarely see or hear faculty theorizing about their discipline or their teaching (trying to solve, for example, the problem of why students are not reading their texts). In short, we see very little of community college teachers at work—preparing lessons, adjusting to the classroom moment, engaging in thoughtful reflection and dialogue.

The image of community college faculty as workhorse teachers is reinforced in a survey done by the Carnegie Foundation. More than 90 percent polled said that they were more interested in teaching than in research. The question was phrased, "Do your interests lie primarily in research or in teaching?" (Boyer 1990, 44). Given the either/or option, the faculty responded in a way that could be hardly surprising. The problem is that the question perpetuates the illogical separation of teaching and research.

In recent years, certain calls have gone out that we reconsider the nature of research and scholarship, and their relationship to teaching (Boyer 1990; Vaughan 1994; Tinberg, "Border-Crossings" 1993). Ernest Boyer, an influential voice, has called for a "scholarship of teaching" (1990, 23). Some have actually argued that we see classroom activities as the fit subject of research in its own right. In composition studies, methods borrowed from fields such as psychology and anthropology—the case study, the oral history, the ethnography—have had an important impact (Kantor, Kirby, and Goetz 1981; Calkins 1985). With the renewed emphasis on teaching (as opposed to research) and on cross-disciplinary learning, such classroom research has inspired a tremendous amount of interest in a short time (Angelo and Cross 1993; Goswami and Stillman 1987; Daiker and Morenberg 1990; Ray 1993).

But such calls have the net effect of further segregating teaching from another, more privileged form of research and scholarship (which Boyer renames "the scholarship of discovery" [17]). Classroom research runs the danger, in my view, of being the things that teachers do when they can't do the "right" kind of research.

More interesting and more profound have been attempts to engage in, to use Henry Giroux's metaphor, "border crossings" (Giroux 1992). By that Giroux means excursions between distinct disciplines and between distinct ways of knowing. The old walls, the old borders between one field and another, simply have lost their usefulness. Giroux argues for a pedagogy centered on "new languages capable of acknowledging the multiple, contradictory, and complex positions people occupy" (21). "Central" to this new pedagogy, he writes, "is the importance of challenging, remapping, and renegotiating those boundaries of knowledge" (26). What this remapping involves is viewing our own disciplines through the lens of another: to wear the difference, as it were, and, in the process, achieve some common ground.

To remap the terrain of knowledge—as ambitious as that might sound—ought to be the goal of teachers who want to engage in scholarship and research. To discover a language that partakes of "border talk" ought to be the means and the end of our inquiry. By "border talk" I mean a language that has currency across the divides between disciplines and institutions, between the local and the global, the practical and the theoretical, the private and the public, the two-year college and the research university. The walls remain, but the translation between becomes the thing.

The work that follows is an attempt at translation, a translation of the work and talk that teachers do. I intend to report what I observed when several colleagues from a variety of disciplines at my community college, along with a group of peer tutors, came together in the summer of 1994 to talk about writing, reading, and knowing. After serving during the previous semester as staff for our college's writing lab, we could now reflect on what we had learned and what we had yet to learn.

My mode of discourse will be as mixed as the border talk heard during those sessions: narratives, journals, and interviews will complement the traditionally academic analysis and argument. The personal will complement the public. As Mary Louise Pratt informs us, personal narratives are as much part of the ethnographic tradition as so-called "objective . . . practices" and much is to be gained from the mingling of the two (1986, 32). Indeed, postmodern ethnographers derive their authority from being part of the picture rather than outside of it (Rosaldo 1993). The truths that emerge from such work, argues James Clifford, are "inherently *partial*—committed and incomplete," but nonetheless authoritative (1986, 7). As I have argued elsewhere, teachers—no matter the institution or discipline—are implicated in their classroom narratives (Tinberg, "Border-Crossings," 9). Decisions that they make—from text selection and syllabi to the arrangement of seats in a circle—influence what happens in their classrooms.

The account that follows will contain many voices, the voices of those engaged and thoughtful colleagues who shared their time and their concerns during our summer sessions. They talked frankly about teaching in their disciplines—and did so with an informed expertise that was truly impressive.

Community college faculty are in a prime position to initiate such an exchange across borders because we live on the borders, as it were. We work in the space between the schools and the universities. In our teaching, we traverse the middle ground between the needs of those who will transfer to the university and those who will enter the working world directly from our classes. Many of us, indeed, have partaken of both the academic and the workaday worlds ourselves. Jerry, from our college's mathematics department, recalled to me the days he drove a truck for a living:

> I drove a truck and made deliveries. These guys called me "teach" even back then, because I had a high school education. Some of them were totally illiterate. By the way, the tags on the bags were color-coded so they could load the right things on the truck.

It is an experience that he continues to draw on as a way to engage his students who are

> out working in machine shops, driving a truck, out on fishing boats. If you can understand the problems that these people are facing right now—and I did it all the way through college, working fifty to fifty-five hours a week when I was in college—if they can understand that you care, they will get something from you. They will understand that your experience is the same as theirs and that you have gone beyond them and that you have something to offer them.

Marlene, a historian, recalls vividly her days working in a factory, which was an attempt to understand the very workers whose lives she was committed to improving. Raised in the upper-middle-class community of Shaker Heights, Ohio, Marlene noted that her father was a high school dropout who had been forced to go to work during the Depression. She observed that she and her family never quite "fit in" in what she called the elitist community where she was raised. The tumultuous political movements taking place in the 1960s showed her that others shared her experience and provided the catalyst for her desire to improve the lot of others.

In a certain sense, we community college faculty are quintessentially postmodern. We possess no single identity, but rather have shifting and blurred identities. Like the subject of postmodern anthropology, we move in a variety of worlds. We are the educational "mestizas," the translatable teachers. I am reminded of what the anthropologist Ruth Behar observes about writing as a woman ethnographer (who happens also to be a Cuban-born Jew):

> The feminist ethnographer is a dual citizen, who shuttles between the country of the academy and the country of feminism. She's an odd kind of bilingual woman. To her subjects she speaks in a tongue bristling with seductive promises that she will not be able to keep. To her colleagues, she must speak in a way that will persuade them that "working" on another woman is a contribution to the discipline she has vowed to serve; they will ultimately judge her work on the basis of how well she can translate the other woman's tongue into a language they can understand. (1993, 297–98)

My goal, in the ethnography to follow, is to shuttle between places in an "odd kind of bilingual" dance—between theory and practice, between teaching and research, between one discipline and another. We will hear discussions ranging from the theoretical question of how we know what we know to the more grounded terrain of what we must do in our classrooms and in our writing centers to improve student writing.

As I sit here at my computer writing this chapter, I am thinking back on what it is like to occupy the space between. A Ph.D. steeped in literary theory and trained in the traditional canon, I strain here and in my classroom to find a language that has currency for theorists as well as for practitioners. I publish, I give papers at professional conferences, and I teach. I work to connect all these activities; I try to translate them across borders. In my professional writing, I try to strike a balance between the public and the private, the academic and the expressive, the abstract and the classroom-based. In my teaching, I seek to use theory as guide to my practice and look to practice to engender theory.

But in bringing theory to discussions of classroom practice at my community college, I run the risk of being seen as "too good" for this place, too high-powered, too Ph.D. (I have actually been told by colleagues that it was only a matter of time before I "moved on.") And as a community college teacher who writes often about my classroom experiences I often run the risk of not seeming scholarly enough to pass muster in professional journals. As I struggle along the borders, I see myself as occupying a "contact zone," the place where, according to Pratt, cultures interact and influence each other. The language that emerges from such a zone "interlock[s] understandings and practices" (1992, 7).

Looking back at our summer workshop, I now see that we were straining to produce that very kind of language ourselves. It was not simply that we were looking to find a common language with which to talk about writing and knowing (as generalists, we felt quite comfortable with the notion). We were also attempting to see whether we could translate to one another the differences that defined us as teachers of psychology, nursing, dental hygiene, literature, history, business, mathematics, and ESL. In my mind, that was the greater challenge.

Essentially, we were to focus, during the workshop, on three questions: What does it mean to write and know in the disciplines? How do we respond effectively to the writing our students do in our courses? And, finally, what do we need to say and do when tutoring students outside of the classroom (when they visit our writing lab)? In answering these questions, we hoped to produce two important documents (which we called "communiqués): a revised statement of "primary traits" or what constitutes "good writing" at our college (building on the statement generated by colleagues at a similar workshop held the previous summer), and a tutoring protocol describing ways to facilitate student learning in a tutoring session.

It was an open question as to whether we would be comfortable talking about discipline-specific ways of writing and knowing. After all, here we were, committed to the community college mission, committed to the mission of general education. Although we were trained to teach our own specialized subject areas, we also saw ourselves as giving students reading, writing, and thinking skills to enable them to flourish in the workplace as well as in academic settings. Does a specialized view of knowledge and knowledge making truly apply to teaching at the community college? we asked ourselves. Are we interested in promoting this specialized view of knowledge or a more generalized or transferable view? "Everything that rises must converge," wryly observed Peter, from the English department. His point was that disciplinary knowledge, if it is to be humane and useful, must offer common ground. And yet, as we talked among ourselves and drew from our own disciplinary perspectives, we asked whether there were disciplinary boundaries or categories that define the work we do, boundaries or categories that perhaps we should make explicit to our students. Marlene, a historian, and Chris, from the psychology department, had the following exchange on the matter:

> *Marlene:* Students will ask, "What do you mean, 'define the Renaissance'?" Well, was it the same for the peasants as it was for the elite? The more I talk the more I elaborate but I am also letting out the the choices for them. . . . I don't have a concept of where I want them to arrive.

Chris: I think you did, from what you were just saying. What you wanted them to do was bring class analysis to answer that question. An economic analysis of the question of the Renaissance. That's actually one of your categories. One of the lenses through which you want your students to see history.

Although class analysis does not belong solely to the study of history, it is for Marlene an important "lens" through which *she* views history. The question for Marlene as an instructor becomes whether she is willing and able to articulate that perspective to her community college students, to lay it out there from the start. Marlene, for her part, construes the act of "giving" her students this kind of information as somehow restricting their choices. She operates from an instinct that most community college teachers have, which is to teach in a way that does not exclude—to produce, in essence, generally educated students. And yet her expectations of students' responses to that assignment seem to be shaped by a class or economic perspective.

Articulating disciplinary ways of knowing, Judith Langer tells us, is no simple or easy task (1992, 83). I might add that it becomes especially challenging at the community college. Not only must we be able to view and understand our discipline's conceptual categories but we must then render them in a language that is useful in the classroom. But even beyond these considerations—as intimidating as they are—is the concern that Kathy, our ESL specialist, raised: "At the two-year college level, how many of our students are actually being asked to write as a historian writes? or asked to write like a psychologist? How much of this is going to be practical at the two-year college?" The need to be "practical," to focus on what works for our students and for the careers and lives they face outside our classrooms, becomes the driving force for a great many of us who teach at the community college. The question then becomes this: Can we at the community college offer knowledge that is *both* specialized and generally useful? We had plenty on our plate.

1 How We Got Here, Where We Want to Go

> I was working fifty hours a week, carrying sixteen or seventeen credits, and it was no easy task.
>
> —Jerry

It is about 1:30 in the afternoon. I am sitting at my computer trying to reconstruct, via my journal, what transpired this morning, day one of our three-week workshop. Already I can see that it will be a difficult task. Leaving aside the trickiness of memory and the disposition to fashion a session to suit my own sense of what ought to have happened, I have to acknowledge from the start that my role during these sessions will be an ambiguous one, shot through with contradictions. As faculty coordinator of our college's writing lab and our summer workshop, I design the workshop agenda, select our readings, and facilitate discussion. At the same time, as a faculty member who also tutors in our writing lab I have a vested interest in the topics that we will discuss. Then, to make matters truly complicated, I am observing, recording, and—now—reconstructing what transpires. I am, in brief, completely implicated in what I am reporting. I make no bones about it: this account will reflect what *I* see and hear, and how I write and think.

But I will also serve as a conduit for the words and thoughts of colleagues. I want to be such right from the start, because in order for readers to care about what it is we say in these weeks, they need to know who we are and how we got here. In interviews, as well as in the workshop itself, I put those questions to my colleagues directly. Each, of course, had applied to become part of the writing lab staff and workshop, but I was interested in relating how and why they became community college teachers in the first place, and what continues to drive them in their work.

I wonder, as I set out to record the stories of my colleagues, whether their accounts are as strangely unpredictable as my own. My own story is anything but linear. When I entered graduate school for the first time, I fully expected to teach at a university. But having been less than successful my first go-round in graduate school, I took the best teaching job I could find (in the late '70s)—a vocational college specializing in training court reporters. There I was, a university-trained white male, teaching grammar, writing, and vocabulary to disadvantaged women of color, women who were determined to make a career for themselves in court reporting. Most of these students worked their way out of poverty and into a very demanding, yet rewarding, profession.

After a year, I returned to graduate school, still hoping to obtain my Ph.D. and teach at a university. Reality would hit like a ton of bricks when I graduated in the early '80s. There were simply very few full-time jobs in English literature (more specifically, British romanticism) at the university level. After a year of teaching part-time sections, I would eventually land a full-time teaching job clear across the globe, in China, where for a year I taught composition and literature surveys to English-language majors at a provincial university. On returning home, I found myself teaching seventh grade in a rural schoolhouse, a job for which I was terribly misfit. After one year, I finally landed a job teaching full-time at a private university. Ironically, after waiting years for just such a job, I came to the conclusion after two years in it that I wanted the chance to teach a more diverse student population than what I found in my university classes. When I saw an opening at a public community college, I resolved to take the plunge.

Pat, who teaches in our dental hygiene program, had taught at the college part-time for many years, taking time off only to raise a family. While working, she returned to college for her bachelor's and, eventually, her master's degrees. When a full-time job opened up in 1990, she took up the challenge. She says that her own very recent experience in school has motivated her to help her own students:

> I had just completed my master's and written paper after paper. I thought maybe I could help somebody else. Maybe I could tell students that it wasn't very long ago that I was in the same boat they are in. . . .

When Pat notes that her experience matches her students' experience, and that this makes her a better teacher, she echoes a refrain of many of her colleagues. One of the most remarkable things about these teachers is how readily they identify with the students they teach, while at the same time recognizing what they can give each of those students. In short, they serve as their students' mentors and, interestingly, their neighbors.

That last point is emphasized by another colleague, Marlene, who suggests that her credibility with her students may have a lot to do with the fact that she lives in New Bedford, the working-class city from which many of her students commute to the college. A former union organizer in a garment factory and a rubber plant, Marlene now teaches history and Western civilization at the college. Long active in political campaigns, Marlene says that her activism has influenced her classroom practice. As she puts it, she adheres to the "possibility of ordinary people becoming historical actors." Creating conditions within her classroom to make that happen, Marlene acknowledges, is a struggle. She would like the workshop to give her strategies to achieve the goal of student empowerment. "I just want students to try to figure things out more," she says, "to seek the great guiding principle: What does this have to do with my life?"

Marlene's twin theme—that students (and "ordinary people") can be agents of change and that the subjects that we teach can be deeply meaningful in the lives of our students—resonates with Diane, a member of our nursing program. Diane came to the community college after ten years of hospital-based nursing. Convinced that nurses need both a clinical and a more generalized (and academic) knowledge, she is committed to a broad view of nursing education or, as she put it in an interview, a "blending of reality with idealism." This view of education has implications for what it takes to be an effective teacher. For Diane, the best kind of teachers are those who have been through the same anxiety about learning as their students. "For myself," Diane says to the group, "the experience of doing nursing was so frightening, so scary. I could see all the responsibility. That's very helpful because I can understand where the anxiety is coming from." What is required is a "generosity of spirit" as well as a reservoir of experience from which to draw. "You would have to have had a variety of emotions [while] sitting in that chair," she says of the effective teacher. In short, for Diane as for so many of us sitting around the table, to teach means to be engaged—in our subject matter, but also in the learning processes of our students.

Jerry, who teaches statistics, takes pride, as we have seen, in bringing to his classroom experiences similar to those of his students. He often draws upon his experience as a full-time worker and full-time student to instruct those students. "I was working fifty hours a week," he says,

> carrying sixteen or seventeen credits all the time, and it was no easy task. So I didn't have a lot of time to study. But what I did to study was constantly write. . . . I had to write and think about the things we were doing. That was the best tool for me—to be able to organize my thoughts, reflect on what took place, to learn.

Writing can also provide a space in which to explore the relationship between students and the work they do. In his statistics course, Jerry has started to ask students to explore, in a reflective way, some of their anxiety about statistics and about math generally.

Such a view of writing would be shared by many on our team, most especially Peter, our English department representative. A prolific author (he has written two well-received biographies of Hemingway) and an energetic teacher, Peter claims a long association with our college, having started to work here in the late '60s as a part-time instructor. Although he has taught at several prestigious colleges and universities, Peter is a local kid who has always been attracted by the opportunity to teach people "from the same neck of the woods" as himself. Hired as a full-time faculty instructor, Peter spent four years at the college before returning to graduate school for his Ph.D. After getting the degree, Peter worked on his first book, supporting himself through part-time employment. The success of that book brought an NEH grant, which, together with more part-time teaching, allowed Peter to write his second book. Peter has returned to our college full-time for a couple of reasons: he has come back to the area in which he has spent so much of his life, and his teaching responsibilities, while heavy, still allow him time to write. For Peter, writing is a passion—both his own writing and the writing that he elicits from his students. "Discover your own voice," he tells his students, "say your own truths." He believes in that completely. And it is a message that he knows his community college students need desperately, since for so long they have been told that their work and ideas "don't matter."

Kathy, from our ESL department, came to our college (after a stint in the Peace Corps), as a bilingual aide, while working at night for her master's. Initially interested in social work, and having spent time working for Catholic charities, Kathy had fully intended to enter graduate school in the field, but because of family considerations had found herself in New England and started teaching at the community college without a master's degree or, as she puts it, "through the back door." Now that she is a full-time instructor, Kathy is intensely interested in the transition that ESL students experience from the time they take courses with other ESL students to the time when they become mainstreamed academically with native speakers of English. The process is extremely complex for them, Kathy observes. A community might throw up roadblocks to prevent outsiders from becoming full-fledged members. She wonders whether other faculty are doing what has to be done to acculturate not only ESL students but also native speakers into the ways of the academic community.

Interestingly, Carol, who comes from our college's business and technologies area, sees her role in much the same light, although the community into which she ushers her students is the business or work setting. Carol worries whether her students will enter the workplace knowing what they need to know and achieving the professionalism required. Carol came to our community college after having taught in middle and high school.

To give our discussions a deeper texture and to enhance our own understanding of what it means for our students to write, I suggest that each of us keep a journal of our experiences in the workshop, and periodically share our responses. I immediately sense collective anxiety at the prospect of keeping a journal in the first place. Although many of us ask our students to keep journals in our classrooms, we are more than a little uneasy about the whole business of journal writing in a classroom (and workshop) setting. Kathy, who teaches ESL, says that she uses a journal in her class to promote her students' fluency in English but acknowledges that there are problems with doing so, most notably the journal's lack of structure and focus and the sometimes disturbingly personal nature of journal responses. Still, Kathy finds journals an effective way to get students' feedback on what it is we are asking them to do for us.

Diane, concurring, says that nursing faculty invite students to comment on the work of instructors. "It's helpful," Diane observes, "in terms of clearing the air." But she worries about the ethical implications of having students comment on a course. "Didn't you have a prejudice," she asks Kathy, "when you asked students to respond?" Diane is concerned that as readers we instructors have a vested interest in what students write. And students are fully aware of what faculty want to hear.

All of us who are sitting around the table see the virtue of having students write often and write in a variety of forms. In theory, we are predisposed to having students write in a form that promotes fluency and that can be done in a nonthreatening way. Our first reading, a piece by Toby Fulwiler on journal keeping, has made us think about the ways that journal writing can do some of these things. As Fulwiler notes, journals have long been used as part of field or clinical observations in a variety of disciplines, from biology to anthropology (1987, 2). Given the wide and diverse experience of this workshop group, we have much to say about the virtues and limitations of journal keeping.

I mention the notion, borrowed from a colleague of mine in the English department, of having students set up a "metatext" in their journals, that is, of asking them to use the journal as a place to reflect on their composing processes and on the written product itself. The journal promotes greater reflection in students and allows them to be more articulate in assessing their own and others' writing.

Jerry, thinking aloud, anticipates using journals as places where his statistics students can explore their anxiety about their subject, setting up a point of reference for later exploration. (As mentioned earlier, he currently has students reflect on their "math anxiety" but in the more formal setting of a graded piece of expository writing.) He sees journals as informal points of entry for his students, a means by which they can connect themselves to a subject that might seem to have little to say to them.

Interestingly, Carol notes that her "co-op" students have as part of their "contract" a requirement to keep a journal. Students enrolled in our college's co-op program split their time between the classroom and the workplace, applying what they learn in the classroom to what they encounter in the workplace. In their journals, students keep a record of what they observe on the job. They often juxtapose, Carol says, their expectations of what they will find with what they in fact experience at the job site. I like the double-sided nature of the journal (like the "double-entry notebook" that Ann Berthoff has recommended [1987]). Those moments when our assumptions meet up with altogether different outcomes can produce wonderful insights.

Diane says that her students must keep journals in part as records of their patients' treatments. As such the writing is evaluated according to fairly straightforward medical standards (to determine that the treatment is "safe"). In addition, students must use their journals to note their observations, evaluating their own behavior. This particular use of the journal seems a powerful learning instrument. Just as Carol's students review previous expectations, so Diane's students engage in a powerful act of revision.

Although Diane does not touch upon it, one other way journals have been used in the health science area has been "to bridge the gap between concepts of professionalism taught in the classroom and the actual clinical experience" (LeBlond 1982, 12). Pat, who teaches in our dental hygiene program, had brought in the LeBlond article, which encourages the use of journals as a place where the ethical dimensions of patient care can be explored. Given the nature of clinical work, students may find themselves, like Carol's students, in situations where what they have learned in the academic setting does not neatly apply to the workplace. More specifically, students might face ethical dilemmas that were never broached in the classroom. The journal might provide a safe environment in which to discuss such issues. To use the journal in that way means, of course, that ethical concerns become as suitable a subject in the classroom as traditional patient care.

In addition to the journals, more preliminaries are brought up: We discuss the objectives for the workshop, to get them on the table. Chief among those objectives is to revisit a document on what makes for "good" writing in the disciplines. From the time that our college first received grant monies to set up our writing lab, it has been a major task of each team of faculty tutors to come to some agreement on those qualities that we consider to be important to effective writing. We wanted to do so in part to guide our own work as tutors in the lab. Having a set of criteria to which to refer when we tutor students about their writing would obviously aid us in our job—and help boost the confidence of those among us who teach in other disciplines than English. It would also ensure that members of the staff were all on the same wavelength.

At the same time, such a document might well have an impact on other colleagues' perceptions of writing and on the position taken by the institution generally on the place of writing in the curriculum. We represent all the divisions of the college, and would, presumably, be able to send word back to our areas as to what we came up with. If all of us in the room can agree first that writing plays a crucial role in our students' learning and second that we can identify certain key components of effective writing, then the rest of the college will fall into line—assigning more writing in their courses but even more important showing a greater awareness of how we should all approach the writing that our students do.

The task of this summer's workshop is in part, then, to build on the work of the previous summer, when the first generation of faculty tutors worked to produce broad guidelines that would be useful in guiding the tutoring that we all were doing in the writing lab. This current team will revisit the previously established criteria in an attempt to refine the list but also to add disciplinary perspectives to it, that is, to inquire whether writing differs in significant ways depending on the discipline that generates it. We intend to engage more of what Kenneth Bruffee calls "boundary discourse," that is, a conversation about the differences of language and inquiry that mark off one discipline from another (1993, 64).

From the start, the idea of constructing a list of "primary traits" of "good writing" did not sit comfortably with me, although I knew that there was support for it in that earlier faculty group. I did not want to see this list—as lists so often do—become the chief authority; I did not want to see the complexity of writing reduced to certain enumerated qualities. I also did not want people to lose sight of the situated nature of writing, that is, the various contexts in which writing is done. Writing expresses the constraints of form, of purpose, and of the very discipline that produces it.

The document produced last summer acknowledged the situatedness of writing while at the same time proceeding to tick off important qualities of writing that apply across disciplines and situations. The result was a kind of schizophrenic document that begins with a caveat:

> The writing lab staff has come to a consensus about "good writing" which we think establishes usable criteria by which to evaluate the writing that we will read in the lab.
>
> A consensus as to "what makes for good writing" should begin with this qualifier: *writing is contextual.* By that we mean that writing depends on the disciplinary context and situation in which it is done. Each discipline does have a distinct set of assumptions about the way knowledge is made and expressed. A student who writes an essay for an English literature course may be ruled by conventions and assumptions quite unlike those that guide the student writing for a history course.

> Nevertheless, we have come to a conclusion on those qualities in writing that cut across areas of expertise and knowledge. We would like these to be considered "primary traits," usable criteria by which to evaluate the many kinds of writing that may come our way.

The document proceeds to identify five broad categories with which to evaluate a piece of writing, accompanied by a brief description:

> **Perspective:** Competent writing must have a strongly stated perspective (this may include what writing teachers call "voice" but could also be described as a point of view) and purpose.
>
> **Audience**: If effective communication is to take place, writing must show some sense of the rhetorical situation (the needs of the audience but also the demands of the form of the writing and the purpose).
>
> **Evidence:** If the intent is to persuade the reader, good writing must marshal evidence or support.
>
> **Logic**: Good writing must have an internal logic and coherence from the localized unit of the paragraph to the structure of the entire work.
>
> **Correctness:** Good writing displays a control of language and tone: grammar, punctuation, and spelling are generally "correct."

As we review the document, we plan to consider the ways in which a discipline might construct or shape any or all of these traits. Is "perspective," for example, so simple a matter when we factor in the expectations of a particular discipline, a discipline that might privilege an "objective" stance? Might "evidence" differ according to the disciplinary lens through which we view it? Might each discipline carry its own distinctive "logic"?

In addition to considering the "situatedness" of our traits, we intend to scrutinize the traits on their own terms. What is "perspective" anyway? And what does it have to do with voice, point of view, and purpose? How do form and purpose shape considerations of audience? Is evidence useful only when the intent is to persuade? Or can it come into play with writing whose purpose is different? How do we talk about evidence, for example, in a narrative or expressive piece?

These questions will be dealt with down the road, when we revisit the traits and rethink the conventions of our own disciplines. But one matter relating to the list will not wait, it seems, and that is the issue of "correctness." Carol, from our business technologies area, questions the use of quotation marks around the word, sensing—quite rightly—that it downplays the relative importance of correct grammar and mechanics. She considers such skills absolutely essential to the work that her students do in the classroom and will do in the workplace. She is appalled by her students' inability to edit their writing, and to demonstrate such skills in any of their courses. "Our students have a hard time transferring their learning from one class to another," she says: "I teach spelling and punctuation in my typing class and they can't write a paper for me in my management class using the same rules."

Chris, who in addition to teaching in the psychology department serves as the writing lab's learning skills specialist, observes that those students are simply not learning those skills. They may be memorizing the rules but they are not allowed to apply them. I add that it makes the most sense to embed editing practice within the composing process, and to give students ample opportunity to apply their editing skills on their own writing. Then they will really learn such skills.

Invariably, this discussion leads us to a truly thorny question: Assuming—as we must at the community college—that many of our students come to us without mastery of language skills, whose responsibility should it be to teach them those skills? Should they be taught in our basic English course? Or in our one required composition course? I beg those questions and ask the group these instead, enlarging the scope to include writing skills generally:

> Should [writing skills] be taught in a class other than English? Should they be taught in any course in which writing is required? If the student is spending some time writing in the courses, should that history teacher, or that nursing teacher, spend some time talking about writing?

The discussion has obviously shifted from a consideration of basic language skills to the much larger question of whose responsibility it is to promote our students' writing generally. Marlene responds by asking Diane, "You're teaching nursing (not writing), right?" Diane can hardly disagree, assuming the separation that Marlene makes between the subject that Diane teaches and the language skills that her students ought to be demonstrating.

In part, the issue has to do with the question of whether all of us at the community college have a shared responsibility to improve our students' writing or whether that should remain solely the responsibility and expertise of the English department. Obviously a sound argument can be made, and Carol more than once has implied this, that the English department ought to take up this task. Certainly, it is a reasonable assumption that, at the very least, students should receive training as editors in their writing courses.

I complicate matters, however, by asking whether there might not be a connection between the tasks we ask of those students and their difficulty with expression. In other words, as they struggle to master our subject's concepts, might students' language skills also be affected—given the connectedness between words and ideas? Might their problems with expression be at least in part due to their inexperience with academic and disciplinary conventions? That question brings us back to one of the tasks before this group, namely, to reflect on the nature of the skills that we expect our students to have when they leave our courses, and our obligations to be explicit as to the expertise we expect of them—explicit to ourselves as well as to our students.

2 Are We Specialists or Generalists?

"[Whether] it's better to live than to die." I said [to my student] that's what [we're] going to discover.

—Peter

It is fast becoming clear to me that all of us sitting around this table have at least this much in common: that the question of what we teach cannot for us be reduced to a simple list of skills, nor our purpose narrowly defined as "instruction." As a group we see our mission as much grander and our role as transformative: we expect to change those students who happen to make their way into our classes, and change them in profound ways.

Historically, community college instruction has sought to avoid the kind of disciplinary specialization that marks university teaching and research. Departments at community colleges have significantly less authority than "divisions" and "programs." The master's remains the essential degree of all instructors rather than the specialized doctorate. The continued presence of career programs requires instructors to be mindful of the ways knowledge can be applied outside their classrooms. "What we teach," then, is not reducible to explicating a literary text, for example, but rather must transcend narrow disciplinary boundaries.

And yet it is easier, perhaps, to say what we don't teach than what we do. If we are not necessarily committed to giving our students specialized knowledge, then what are we giving them, exactly? Marlene gets the ball rolling when she tells us about the "turning point" in her teaching, her involvement in a critical thinking seminar followed by a change in her classroom practice. She begins by talking about the way, in those early days, she taught the Middle Ages:

> I would ask a question and the students had to be woken out of a daze. It was really frightening. I consider myself a good lecturer. [Yet] they were so passive. . . . I know a couple of times when I put them into groups how they would come alive. I made a decision after the first semester that I wasn't going to do [just] lecturing anymore. . . .

Even as Marlene would shift more of the responsibility for learning onto her students, she rightfully claims as the subject of her course the "great guiding principles." That is, she regards what she teaches her students as life-enriching, rather than simply all they need to know about the Middle Ages.

At this point Peter offers a classroom narrative of his own. He recalls a student's walking up to him on the first day of his American literature class and telling him that her brother had advised her that the class was a waste of time. She wanted to know why she should take the course. Peter recalls:

> It was after the riots in L.A., and a kid [on TV] was talking about a drive-by shooting. I don't know if he had participated in one but the interviewer said, "What if it had been your children?" And the kid said, "So what? It's better to die than to live."

Peter reverses that statement. "It's better to live than to die," he tells the student:

> That's what we're going to discover. Some of the best minds in American literature can give us an affirmation that will make us believe that it is better to live than to die. And that's what I'm going to try to teach in this course: Can we give that kid some answer?

We are all touched by Peter's response, eloquently and passionately expressed. He reminds us that what we hope to accomplish in our classrooms must be bigger than a narrow shopping list of "what students need to know." Instead what we ought to be doing is reflecting on what drew us to our specialties in the first place and trying to impart the wisdom given to us by our study to those who enter our classrooms. "When doing an introduction to literature," says Peter, "I tend to pursue those things that I myself need in my life."

Peter's story prompts us to consider questions that we too rarely ask of ourselves: Why should students take our courses? What exactly do we expect our students to leave with? Diane amends the question, or supplements it, this way: "Why take this course from *you?* What is it that *you* give to the course . . . that would make the course more rewarding?" Diane's revision hardly surprises me, given who we are and where we presently teach. In restating the question this way, Diane nudges us to remember that whatever happens in the classroom derives in large measure from the quality of our teaching. We are teachers first and foremost. We bring something to our subjects and our classrooms that is indispensable if students are to learn.

But what is it that we teach exactly? What are the methods of inquiry peculiar to our subjects and disciplines? These are difficult questions for us to answer. In one of our readings for today's session, Lee Odell puts the problem this way: "Some of these ways of knowing may become so internalized that it is difficult to bring them to conscious awareness in order to help someone else understand them" (1992, 97). All of us have been trained in the methods of a particular specialty, whether in nursing, in mathematics, in English, in office management, in history, or in psychology. But to be able to articulate those methods—to render them explicit to ourselves and to our students—there's the rub. Moreover, as has already been seen, many people sitting around this table may resist the pressure to highlight what separates us and instead want to build on "common ground." Diane, in fact, tells us about listening to a keynote address at a recent conference that she attended. The speaker was Kenneth Bruffee ("Keynote," 1993), who for years has written and spoken eloquently about collaborative learning. Diane remembers that Bruffee, in describing the various obstacles faced by tutoring centers, noted the peculiar divisions within the academy. "Picket fences," he called them, structures erected to keep the barbarians out:

> The whole focus [of Bruffee's talk] was that the language of the profession is the picket fence that keeps out the uninitiated. . . . as you go along they give you more of the language so that you understand what they are saying.

Teaching as we do at a public, open-admissions community college, all of us feel some discomfort talking about the "uninitiated" and the kind of exclusiveness inherent in the disciplines-as-picket-fences metaphor. And yet all of us, whether we like to admit it or not, are among the "initiated" or, put another way, all of us have acquired a specialty or expertise that our students have not.

In the semester preceding our workshop, as part of our weekly staff meetings, we had begun the process of "thinking about our disciplinary thinking." All of us had written down "what makes for good writing in our disciplines." I had made the request because I thought that an increased awareness of disciplinary concerns might improve our performance as tutors in the writing lab as well as enhance the writing assignments in our own classes, and that such concerns would amount to evidence of the way a discipline represents itself in writing. Disciplinary writing and reading, as Charles Bazerman has observed, are "highly contextualized social actions," symbolic activities with a distinctive rhetorical character (1988, 22). The results of our efforts had brought to the surface the group's mixed feelings about discipline-specific ways of knowing. Some of us were more comfortable than others with the idea of articulating disciplinary differences. For example, Mia, a part-time philosophy and writing instructor who tutors in our writing lab (and who, alas, couldn't attend our summer workshop), seems at ease when writing about her field's "discourse" (take note, however, of the way she begins with commonality):

> Of course, philosophy recognizes the writing traits which are universally characteristic of coherent written communication. However,

philosophy is no different from other disciplines in that it works from a distinct agenda. All philosophical discourse needs to begin with an inquiry. The writer then must engage him- or herself into the discourse which necessarily surrounds the inquiry. (For example, an inquiry into the existence of truth must first define truth rather than assume universal agreement on its meaning). The discourse should flow from a logical progression of thought wherein claims, arguments, and explanations are developed from empirical or a priori evidence. In addition, veteran philosophers (assuming that there is such a thing) are expected to employ the terminology of the discipline and to display a degree of scholarship in the subject matter surrounding the inquiry.

Mia lets it be known that her discipline's distinctiveness depends on more than just a specialized vocabulary. More fundamentally, she looks at philosophical discourse as a form of inquiry and argumentation.

Interestingly, Kathy, representing the extradisciplinary field of ESL, speaks most insistently on recognizing different ways of knowing: "I think . . . that it is very important that we allow these students to maintain the beauty of their individual voices and linguistic styles." She goes on to describe Robert Kaplan's scheme of "contrastive rhetoric," which distinguishes among cultures in terms of thinking processes and, by extension, the linguistic expressions of those processes (1966, 15). Kathy's point is that we need to respect such differences. She acknowledges, however, that, for all the need to retain their cultural styles, the fact remains that success for her students is measured by how well they write and think classroom English.

Marlene, in responding to what makes for "good writing" in history, chose in her earlier statement to focus on generalized or generic aspects of writing. A good history paper, she asserted, needs a "good introduction," a "clear argument with evidence," and a clear point of view. When she is asked, now, to describe to a student why she should take her course, Marlene goes much deeper, revealing some of her own (and the group's) conflicting notions of writing in the disciplines:

> I think what I'm trying to do in my course is to give my students what it is like being a historian, not with the view that they will be historians, but with the view that there are certain things everyone should do, and that is to be very aware of your sources, where you get information, [be] aware of the authors and their perspectives, when they were born, the social classes they came from, the influences on their lives. You look at the arguments they make. Are they insightful? Do they make sense? Are the inferences that are drawn credible? That's the kind of thing that I want my students to get out of it . . . and to transfer that to other things in life. When they pick up the newspaper every morning, [then,]they realize that it is a profit-making organization and what they read may not be the whole story.

Marlene wants, in fact, to give her students a sense of what it means to be a historian, her protests notwithstanding. And it is clear to me that for Marlene history amounts to more than just a record of the facts. She sees history as the site of conflicting opinions and debatable inferences. She sees history as argument and as a construction of events as shaped by the writers' personal histories. At the same time, however, Marlene insists that the skills she is imparting to her students are transferable to "other things in life," and not specific to historical writing and thinking. The apparent discomfort that Marlene feels with seeing herself as a specialist imparting specialized knowledge is something that many of us in this room and in the community college feel: Are we teachers or specialists? That question implies, of course, that disciplinary knowledge has little to do with what we say and how we act in the classroom.

As if to highlight that point, Peter's account of "good writing in an English class" seems strangely acontextual. For him, good writing in English must have a "voice, a dramatic voice, the feeling that an honest-to-God person is speaking to you. . . . There's a poetic economy to good writing. . . . Good writing is re-creative. There's a vividness to it, the surprise of fresh imagery." Interestingly, the writing done in English becomes for Peter a kind of writing that can be taught regardless of the discipline that generates it.

In contrast, my own account of writing in English begins as a description of my training in writing about poems, that is, a kind of writing more directly rooted in the academy:

> I was trained to write what is called an "explication of the text." By that I mean a close, well-reasoned discussion of what a poem has to offer: from the twists and turns of the argument to the texture of language and patterns of sound. When I was in graduate school, New Criticism (which was at least thirty years old by then), still provided the means by which to explicate a poem: treat the poem on its own terms, as a discrete unit; apply whatever tools the discipline offers (from parsing verse to reading for irony and back); and *never* confuse the writing and the writer, *please.*

But that was then and this is now. I write that I have since then moved "beyond" the New Critical approach:

> Instead I ask my students—especially in an introductory literature course—to connect the poem with their lives. That doesn't mean ignoring the text but rather seeing the poem as expressive of the world. In addition, I am more likely in discussing a poem to consider the social and cultural pressures that helped to produce it.

As I think about the "change," I can see that, while I no longer confine my response about a poem to the text on the page, I am nevertheless

talking about a rather specialized kind of writing and thinking (and reading), and that the writing I describe emerges from the reading. I focus in
my statement on writing that is situated within a particular disciplinary
context.

Returning to the workshop, I am surprised, in the light of Peter's
acontextualized account of good writing, to hear him saying that he prefers to see each discipline as applying "particular metaphors . . . ways of
speaking, actions. . . . a way of structuring reality in order to get at a particular meaning." At this point, Marlene, the historian, rightly reminds
us that what we call disciplines were not considered so before the late
nineteenth century, when the German university model was adopted in
this country. Having said this, she presses us further to make this entire
discussion more concrete. What kinds of differences are we talking about,
anyway, she asks?

To try to render our discussion more concrete, the group turns to a
passage from our previous night's reading, in which Lee Odell (1992) talks
about "context-specific ways of knowing." To illustrate the distinct demands a discipline may make on student work, Odell draws upon student
reports from a mechanical engineering assignment. The assignment is to
"design a mechanical advice that can be used to develop the 'technological awareness' of fifth-, sixth-, and seventh-grade students" (93). One group
of students decides to design a "mock wind tunnel" to test the aerodynam-
ics of model cars, and Odell pulls out two design descriptions done by
members of the group. Their differences could not be more clear-cut. One
begins, "The mock wind tunnel is designed to demonstrate, in a crude
manner, the behavior of air flow over a child-size model of an automo-
bile that the child assembles himself" (93). Another student writes the
description in a very different way: "The mock wind tunnel consists of a
tube 46" long, 3 1/4" ID [interior diameter], 3 1/2" OD [outer diameter].
The tube is supported at each end and in the middle" (93). When asked
which of the two he prefers, the instructor chooses the latter because, he
says, while the first provides a useful overview, the details given in the second show that the student had indeed designed the product, and provides the necessary information to convince readers "that it would work"
(95).

Are these differences significant or, rather, is the second example more
typical of writing in engineering design? Kathy prefers to restate the question to "What were the expectations of the writing [assignment]?" She sees
the difference as purely a matter of audience. The first student, in providing a view of the big picture, simply addresses a different audience from
what the teacher has in mind, an audience with less technical expertise.
But, of course, that merely begs the question of what the student needs

to do and know in order to satisfy the instructor's expectations. Those expectations seem rather specific to engineering design (to show "that it would work").

Kathy's discomfort with the notion that particular disciplines set up particular expectations becomes quite obvious in an exchange between her and Peter (who now has become associated in Kathy's mind with disciplinary "picket fences"):

> *Peter:* By being true to your discipline, you make the work most relevant to your students. . . . I think the world is best perceived through one window [that is, of our particular discipline]. I think if you look through that one window as best as you can, you give your students . . . the truth that you have.
>
> *Kathy:* You said you have to give them what you know, the truth as you see it, but you also have to give them what's relevant. So [Howard's] not focusing on the literary terms is not changing the mission [of the college].

Kathy's last comment was in response to my own admission that in my introductory literature course I no longer require my students to use conventional literary terms. It is no longer important to me that my students parse a line of verse. I draw on their own experiences as a way to engage the text. As a consequence, I ask, "Am I teaching my students something outside my discipline, for the sake of 'relevance'? And if so, is my course somehow less an English course?"

Peter's metaphor of the disciplinary "window" is a useful one for our group. Indeed, it is most revealing, since it suggests that although we may see the world through our distinctive disciplinary perspectives we may not always be aware of the frame or pane itself. We need to be more aware, I think, of what frames our knowledge and our teaching.

To that end, I ask Pat, from our dental hygiene area, what specific skills she wishes her students to have when they finish their program of study. "Making connections between observations," she replies. She continues:

> In an oral exam, making connections [between] an observation [and] what you've read in textbooks about conditions that might apply, [for example] viral or chemical burn. Bleeding or poor gum tissues can be the result of many things. Students need to be able to look at it and put the pieces of knowledge together, visually observing what they are seeing, connecting it to what they already know.

Knowledge, in other words, is made when what we know and what we observe come into conflict. Diane, from the perspective of nursing, calls such knowledge-making the "so-what hypothesis," that is, taking what we agree to be the "reality" and juxtaposing it to the observed condition of a patient and the appropriate behavior of the nurse: So what if that text-

book case happens? What are the implications of the condition for patient and practitioner?

Such questions lead us invariably to the idea that an observer's perspective—the voice from the ground, so to speak—plays an important role
in the construction of knowledge. What I'm hearing from Pat and Diane
brings me to speak about what I've read in Kenneth Bruffee and Richard
Rorty about the socially constructed nature of reality, the view that knowledge is made by the consent of a community of learners (Bruffee 1984;
Rorty 1979).

Marlene observes that "at any moment there are multiple truths." She
points to historical texts that disregard the perspectives and truths of what
she calls "ordinary people," the forgotten or silent figures. "Revolutions,"
she observes, "are not made by men at the top but by millions." Marlene's
insistence in her courses that students know something of "class interests"
makes clear her particular perspective on historical events, the lens
through which she views the past. Generally speaking, says Chris, we all
rely on various "categories" with which to organize our perceptions.

Chris makes that remark in part because of Marlene's comments but
also because of an anecdote that I had shared with the group. I had had
a conversation with a colleague from our chemistry department, who had
his students report on all the things they saw when observing a candle
burning. They were to begin by writing down what they expected to see
when a candle is burning. Then they were to light a candle and observe
in as much detail as they could what they saw. The teacher told me that
some students reported roughly fifty independent, observable details. Like
Pat's and Diane's students, these students learned in part by juxtaposing
what they expected and what they in fact observed. But, more profoundly
perhaps, they engaged in a kind of seeing that may very well be specific
to a particular community. Were the students given certain categories of
observation, certain habits of seeing to which the rest of us don't have
access? Marlene, similarly, sees her role as getting students to see the "patterns" of history, discrete categories with which she organizes historical
events. Chris makes the important point that disciplines have clear, de-
finable boundaries, although overlap exists. Distinct lines separate physics from chemistry—ways of observing and testing phenomena.

Interestingly, Diane remarks that some teachers are reluctant to render those expectations explicit in the writing tasks that they assign their
students. "Sometimes," she notes, "it's almost as if we are afraid of giving
away the secret." Somehow—through osmosis perhaps—students must
find that secret in order to become successful, but there is precious little
explicit guidance. Marlene admits that she is not explicit enough in the
instructions that she gives to her students, out of fear of "giving away" the

assignment. When she asks them, as we have seen, to define the Renaissance, she would like them to discover that a variety of perspectives, including that of the peasants, exists on the subject. "The more I talk [about such perspectives], the more I elaborate," she says, "but I am also setting out the choices for them." Chris disagrees. He feels that the economic analysis of history—the lens through which she views it—might simply guide Marlene's students. "They're still going to have to struggle to analyze," he reminds us.

As I reflect upon Marlene's concern, I see that in some ways she is closer to the crux of the matter than any of us. She connects the special expertise that marks us as members of a disciplinary community with the authority that it confers on us. We teachers have the knowledge; our students simply do not. Although Marlene would like her students to discover that knowledge, our assisting with explicit guidance may indeed be seen as "giving away" the very stuff that buttresses our authority in the classroom. For Marlene, then, the issue becomes whether we should "lower our standards" in order to get the work that we would like from our students. In fact, that is less the issue than whether we are prepared to welcome the outsider into our knowledge community and whether we are prepared to assist in that process.

3 Our Ways of Reading and Knowing

Doesn't every piece have a special argument?

—Marlene

Partly as a way to test the assumption that each of us belongs to distinct discourse communities, I suggest that we bring in writing that reflects our own particular areas of interest and experience. But I do so for other reasons as well. For one, I want us all to experience the role of the expert. In one sense we are familiar with that role. Every time we stand before our students, we, and they, assume that we possess authoritative and expert knowledge. And yet it is the unique plight of two-year college teachers that our very expertise undergoes continual challenge—not by students but by the institutional culture of the two-year college. Given the comprehensive nature of the community college mission, faculty at the two-year college level are encouraged to view themselves as experts in teaching rather than experts in teaching a subject. Attempts to define ourselves as both expert teachers and expert scholars too often meet with indifference or outright discouragement. As in any discussion that unnaturally separates teaching from research (which must include scholarship), this debate goes against what we all know by common sense to be true: that what we teach is connected to how we teach and that the "what" constantly changes as our disciplines change.

But beyond acknowledging our own expertise in our subjects, another result may come from sharing disciplinary texts: Perhaps we will feel the discomfort that comes from being outside a knowledgeable community and from not knowing how to read the map of another discipline's text. I am, frankly, hoping that such discomfort occurs. It may cause us to reflect on the process that each of us has gone through to become part of our disciplines' conversations, a process that many of our students struggle with in our own classrooms.

What we bring in comprises an interesting medley. Some of us have brought in journal articles, others have brought excerpts from textbooks and other professional publications. Pat presents us with an American Dental Hygiene Association publication called "The Student Journal: Its Use in Teaching Ethics in Dental Hygiene Programs" (LeBlond 1992). Written in accessible, nontechnical language, the piece uses some of the literature about journal keeping in other fields (most notably the work of Toby Fulwiler) and applies it to the field of dental hygiene instruction.

Diane brings in an article titled "Are You up to Date on Diabetes Medications?" from the *American Journal of Nursing* (Kestel 1994). Written by a teaching nurse for working nurses, the article makes distinctions among various modes of diabetes treatment, and makes reference to various studies done in the field to make its point. Carol brings in an article on "Development of Cases for Business Report Writing Classes," which details a specific teaching assignment using the case study approach as a basis for research and analysis. Drawing upon research on writing by corporate employees, the authors claim that analytical reports are indeed expected in the corporate environment. Interestingly, the authors implicitly recognize developments in composition when they recommend that teachers focus on the "writing process rather than on the researching process" and that students ought to work together to share their findings (Nelson and MacLeod 1993, 37, 39).

Clearly, these pieces say a lot about us. All the writing samples, while situated in particular disciplines, are accessible to the outsider. We—all of us—want to find common ground; the urge is very deep in us. We all feel discomfort with those disciplinary "picket fences" that Kenneth Bruffee mentions ("Keynote," 1993). We are, after all, *community* college teachers. And yet each of us is a product of specialized training. Our thinking, the ways we read, write, and talk—all to some degree reflect that training.

That becomes clear when we look at a particular piece, Diane's piece on treatment for diabetes. The pretext for our discussion of that work is to get at how a particular discipline uses sources—that is, how someone writing in an area makes reference to, and builds on, already established knowledge in that subject. More profoundly, we are interested in discovering how writers position themselves vis à vis that established knowledge. How do they establish a point of view next to authors whom they cite? As writing lab tutors, we often express our frustration at students' inability to quote from, and cite, sources. Too often we read "research" writing from students that amounts to a crazy quilt of quoted passages, with very little evidence of the students' own perspective (Meyer and Smith 1987, 245). But we also realize just as often that students rarely get classroom instruction in how to do genuine research, a crucial aspect of which is to know how to carve out a point of view and to weave that point of view together with the opinions of experts. Philosophically, the challenge for writers—novice and expert—is to understand that language operates referentially, and that particular discourse communities expect that writers make new knowledge while acknowledging the established, conventionally held knowledge. Claims need to be situated within or next to accepted belief. As one example, consider what it means to research and write in science:

> An individual does well for him[-] or herself, his or her social net-
> work, and for his or her claims, by doing good science; that is, by cre-
> ating representations of some stability and power when held against
> the accumulated and future experience of the community. (Bazerman
> 1988, 190)

Of course, writers within such a community need to have confidence
(which means "power") enough to make their claims even as they survey
the stable knowledge of their community. Our students more often than
not lack the confidence to assume the stance of "expert" next to the received knowledge that they research. They often fail to establish a point
of view from which to mount an argument.

Interestingly, when we begin to discuss the piece that Diane has brought
us on diabetic treatment, we argue among ourselves about the meaning
of that very phrase "point of view." More precisely, some of us wonder
whether the piece indeed has any point of view at all. Kathy begins the
"argument about argument" by separating what she sees as the "thesis" of
the piece from any "point of view" (which she has difficulty finding). As
she puts it, the "thesis" of the piece is, "You need to keep up with medications." The point is made at the end, in a "classically organized essay." Peter
concurs by saying that the article offers "exposition rather than argumentation." In other words, Kathy and Peter see very little of an argumentative edge, very little of an agenda propelling the writer and the piece itself.

Marlene, however, reads the same article through very different lenses.
She asks, "Doesn't every piece have a special argument?" In asking that
question, Marlene posits a view of language (and of writing and reading)
that is quite at odds with the view of others in the group. In part, she reflects her own training as a historian: seeing history as a sifting of interpretations or counterarguments (Walvoord and McCarthy 1990, 99). For
Marlene, historians don't simply provide the facts but rather their interpretation of the facts. Moreover, Marlene sees a text and a writer coming
out of a "certain tradition." She sees writing generally as constructed by
the world external to the page. Regarding the piece on diabetes, Marlene
immediately latches onto the writer's "point of view": "She is definitely
within the tradition of Western-style medicine. She is not looking at ho-
listic medicine, at acupuncture, at homeopathy. . . . She's accepting only
a [Western] orthodox medicine." If we believe, along with reader-response
theorists, that a text is "made" in part by the readers who come to it, then
Marlene's reading may be seen as her shaping of that text.

Diane complicates our reading even further. She notes that the writer
is herself a nurse educator rather than a physician. "Physicians," she says,
"just look at the diseases":

They never figure out who has the disease, how it affects [the patient]. For example, a fifteen-year-old boy is going to be a lot more difficult to handle than a thirty-five-year-old man who has a routine pattern of exercise. Doctors are very hesitant to say you're a college student, you're not going to be eating at home so we have to look at the cafeteria. . . . Nurses have always done that because the physicians will prescribe. Then we will say to the patient, Did you understand that? Can you do that? . . . You find out this is a person.

The writer's perspective affects the writing itself in rather obvious ways, Diane says. She points to the references to particular cases and names: "Benny Brewster, 15 . . . was young, lean, and quite abruptly ill" (Kestel 1994, 48). The writing becomes compelling in its concreteness and in its humanity.

All these findings notwithstanding, Peter persists in stating that while the piece exhibits a writer's point of view it does not have a "thesis," which he defines as a "sharp, clear, definite position": "She's just giving us information. She's not really proving anything." Peter does not want us to "reduce point of view to prejudice," as he puts it: "I think point of view can mean everything you bring to a subject. It's your attention, your attitude, your way of looking at things. . . . Thesis is narrower."

The sparks between Marlene and Peter now begin to fly:

Marlene: [reading aloud what she feels to be the writer's point:] "I want to inform you of the latest update in. . . ." Second, there is a break now with the past practice of treating diabetes, with the new, innovative method being basically better than the old ways of doing it.

Peter: You're going outside the article. Look, [let's assume that someone says] this is the way to draw blood and then they give you how to do it. And somebody else says I think there's another way to draw blood that's more effective. Argumentation would be, "Drawing blood is the first step in any physical." That's an argument.

Diane then jumps in: "I disagree with you, Peter, because of the title. When she asks the question, 'Are You up to Date [on Diabetes Medications]?, [she implies] that people are not up to date. I think it's a very provocative question."

What's happening here? Suddenly those "picket fences" that Diane mentioned earlier are being erected, with Peter and Carol (who believes, with Peter, that the article is an "informational piece") on one side and Marlene and Diane on the other, with Kathy seemingly uncertain as to the side to which she belongs. Are we stumbling over semantics or are these differences deep-seated? To get at an answer I suggest that we either reexamine our terms, like thesis or argument—perhaps getting away from using them altogether—or use altogether different words. What if we use the word "purpose" instead? I ask. Peter immediately responds by saying that the word is "so general." The argument about argument then branches out to become an argument about modes of discourse:

> *Howard:* There has to be a motive for writing.
>
> *Peter:* It usually is broken down into exposition, argumentation, description, and narration.
>
> *Howard:* But I don't buy into those distinctions anymore. In my mind there is an interconnectedness. And when we buy into the modes we're saying that these are nicely sealed off.
>
> *Peter:* I wrote two biographies that are straight narratives, the whole thing implied.
>
> *Diane:* You didn't have any arguments?
>
> *Peter:* No. You are totally blurring the distinctions.
>
> *Howard:* No, I'm not. I said "interconnected."

In truth, I am "blurring the distinctions." Peter is right. Perhaps I am bringing to this discussion all that I have been told about "blurred genres"—postmodern views of forms and modes as overlapping—and about the "situatedness" of language (Geertz 1983; Clifford 1986). To talk about a narrative as if it could proceed without "argument" seems misguided. Kathy offers a very astute comment about the slippery slope of an insular and formal approach to writing: "That's the danger of assigning a form. If you have your students do an argumentative paper, then you're having the form drive the message." That form, she may as well add, exists only in the classroom—a fact that only adds to our students' confusion when faced with such a task.

His protestations notwithstanding, even Peter will acknowledge that in a narrative "the whole thing [can be] implied." That latter comment would suggest that what Peter is getting at is the difference in levels of explicitness. A writer may provide exposition explicitly but may also promote a point or agenda implicitly.

At this point, despite having all my postmodern sensibility firmly in place, I nevertheless cannot help blurting out, "Can we not agree on what the damn thing is saying?" Does our argument about argument make it impossible to state the gist of the piece? Marlene reminds us of Diane's reading of the writer's point: that the latest innovations in diabetes treatment should be chosen over more conventional therapy. But Peter insists that if this is true the writer is just "making an assertion": "If she were making an argument she would have to marshal evidence, saying this is the quality of the new medicine. This is how it is better than the old, back and forth, back and forth." I am glad that Peter says this because in asking "Where's the beef?" he is forcing us to go back to the text and to become close readers of the piece. He forces us to go to the writer's words (and to reexamine our own). If we were explicating the text, we would have to provide the evidence for what we say. Diane and Marlene have stated that there is in fact a kind of argument here in the contrast between treatments, and therefore they must show where in the text they see an argument, a line being drawn.

And they proceed to do so. Diane, like a good, close reader of a text, points to a passage on page 50 where the writer refers to "outdated but still common" kinds of therapy. She reads that line to mean "still common" with doctors "[but] not with the people who are reading the article." Moreover, Diane notes, the writer observes that the traditional treatment given to Benny, the fifteen-year-old patient, "may not," in the words of the writer, "provide adequate overnight glucose coverage" (Kestel 1994, 51). Diane is crafting a very nice argument of her own, of course. She is providing evidence, methodically and thoughtfully, that the writer uses a language of critique. The writer, Diane is saying, makes judgments and weighs treatments.

This discussion makes me think of the difficult task of showing our students how to master a critical language, both as writers and as readers. If a room full of experienced teachers and readers can respond in such varied ways to a writer's critique, and if such a critique can appear in such an unobtrusive form, what chance have we to make our students sensitive to such language? Taking up this subject, Jerry, who has been quiet during this "argument about argument," tries to look at the article from the student's frame of reference. Students, he says, would be guided in their "translation" of the article by their teachers' instructions. If their teachers want them to "find an argument" they will find it. I can tell that for Jerry Diane's reading of the article would make little sense to our students. But, of course, that is hardly surprising. Those students would not bring Diane's breadth of experience to the text. Indeed, very few in this room are bringing that kind of experience to their reading of the piece.

What do we do then with that word "argument," when all is said and done? Peter himself suggests that we "get rid of that." He asks us to look at the "narrative quality" of the article. By that he refers to the effective use of anecdote or case studies. He sees a dramatic quality in the writing: essentially, the willingness of the writer to tell stories. And to be concrete. He asks us to consider such stories as powerful evidence which the author uses to support her convictions. Once, Peter tells us, a student apologized to him for "being anecdotal" in a paper. He said to her, "Why?" We, in fact, all know the answer to that one: teachers have been notorious in their resolve to take students, and what they consider the "merely" personal or subjective, out of their writing.

Now, it seems that Peter and the rest of the group are moving together at the center: agreeing that writers can indeed present a thoughtful point of view without contriving a full-fledged argument. But just when you think you have Peter, he surprises you. The very next day, Peter brings in a reading himself. Taken from *Atlantic Monthly*, the piece is entitled "The Sex-Bias Myth in Medicine" (Kadar 1994). It is a contentious and provocative piece, for sure. Peter is clearly saying to us, "You want an argumentative piece of writing? Try this on for size." The writer begins with a long passage detailing accusations from women's groups that women have for too long been ignored by the medical field, that their needs have not been met. Peter points to the writer's skillful use of "rhetoric":

> I think the introduction is really important. He gets the reader saying yes and almost gives the reader the sense that this is just another piece, a predictable piece, and then presents a thesis which turns it all around. . . . it suggests a whole strategy to draw you in . . . and surprise you.

The thesis that is finally given amounts to the view that while there is indeed a sex bias in medicine, that bias favors women and not men. The writer proceeds to critique, with some vigor, previous studies on gender bias in health. But Peter does not give us the whole article, nor do we see the list of works cited. As Pat noted, "It would make the article more credible if [we] could look at [the references]." Marlene concurs, taking some offense at what she sees is the trivialization of "the other side" in this piece. She calls for argument that is "principled."

But Peter is making a larger point here. He knows full well that balance and logic are important ingredients in an effective appeal to change people's minds. Yet he also puts some stock in expressiveness, on emotion. Classical rhetoricians, he tells us, put stock in the "emotional appeal, the ethical appeal, and the logical [appeal]." An argument might then draw upon all three.

Marlene reminds us all how cold and bloodless is so much of our students' writing—especially when drawing upon external sources. How do we encourage students to stake out, and support, an opinion—emotionally, ethically, and logically? Can writers be both passionate and objective, asks Diane? Peter responds by drawing upon Wordsworth's view of poetry as the spontaneous overflow of powerful emotion, but emotion recollected in tranquility. "There should be passion," he says, "but passion always passed through" thoughtful reflection. It is of course one thing for students to write passionately on matters close to their own experience, but what about the French Revolution? asks Marlene. How do I encourage passionate argument in history?

4 Using History

Students believe there is only one story.

—Marlene

When Marlene expresses her desire that students write passionate histori-cal argument, I cannot help thinking of two assumptions underlying that desire: that ideas can be passionately held and expressed and that such academic work has significance beyond the classroom exercise. At the two-year college, where the time to reflect—to engage the world of ideas—may indeed be seen as a "luxury" afforded to the few, the academic com-ponent of the comprehensive mission can be given short shrift. So often we overhear students as well as colleagues refer to what is needed in "the real world," a world quite different, apparently, from that of the classroom. So often we two-year college teachers, imbibing the utilitarian milieu of our institutions, view our teaching in purely utilitarian terms: giving stu-dents workplace skills or giving them credits to enable them to transfer smoothly to four-year schools. The notion that ideas (and scholarship) matter, not only for what they can do in the world but for their own sake, gets lost amid our students' goal of obtaining a well-paid job and our own well-intentioned efforts to serve the community's practical needs.

Surely, any effort to foster the academic culture of the two-year college must begin with the view that the intellectual enterprise poses no threat to the comprehensive mission of the college. Nor should intellectual work be seen as trivial next to vocational and transfer functions. As I listen to colleagues around this table debating how we read and know—and do-ing so with considerable passion and conviction—I feel confident that for these teachers classrooms can be places where ideas catch fire.

But what does it mean exactly to be passionate about history? Diane asks, "Can there be passion if there is objectivity?" Don't historians look at events through the clear medium of intellect rather than through the unreliable filter of emotion? Marlene has of course all along presented a view of history as a tissue of perspectives, an amalgam of historians' bi-ases and the biases of their times. But what does such historical writing look like? We clearly need an example or model to anchor us—much as do our students, who so often travel through our courses without ever seeing the way a historian or a sociologist really writes and works.

Marlene obliges us with the introduction to a class text entitled *Life-lines from Our Past* (Stavrianos 1992). She chooses to draw from this particular book because it has had a huge impact on her view of history. Specifically, she says, she has been influenced by the writer's view of history not as steady progress (which, according to Marlene, would express a Judeo-Christian perspective only) but as recursive. In other words, the writer may, for example, look at hunter-gatherer societies in all their complexities and, in certain respects, note the advantages of such societies relative to our own.

It becomes obvious as well that Marlene admires the author's view of history's usefulness. Rather than see history as merely predictive, the author offers a complicated notion of his discipline's "relevance":

> History deals with human beings whose actions can hardly be predicted at all, much less with the certainty that a chemist can predict what will happen when element A is combined with element B. . . . Its usefulness is not in being predictive, but in providing a framework for considering past and present—a framework that will not foretell what is to come, but that can reveal the human flexibility and human potentiality that is our legacy. (12)

We can learn from the past and become a better society, Marlene says in summing up the writer's premise, but we cannot assume that such will happen without studying and understanding history. Nor is history locked in a causal scheme free of human agency.

The framework that the writer provides is astonishingly personal. "All macrohistory is autobiography," he begins, and proceeds to describe the "roots" of this history in his own upbringing during the Depression (3). Having worked early in his life as a waiter in a skid row restaurant, the writer recounts his impressions of the great disparity between the customers that he served and the affluence present elsewhere in Vancouver and in British Columbia generally. Taking his skid row restaurant experience as his "university," the writer roots his schooling and later academic career in that earlier experience and commits his life to exploring the "gap between official rhetoric and the social reality" (5). "The role of a historian," he writes, "should be to cast light on the origins of that gap" (5). Just as the writer has traced his own particular "lifeline," so he intends to analyze the lifelines of larger human communities, as they break into three groups (kinship, tributary, and capitalist societies).

Marlene assigns this introductory chapter in her early modern history course to demonstrate the historian's "bias":

> I wanted [my students] to say he had a bias. A bias for students means something bad. . . . We had a discussion of what I thought was his bias. [I said that] he sees things in terms of the many. What are the interests of the many? Why aren't the needs of the many being met by the few?

But the "many" in this room are not ready to go even that far with Marlene. We are struggling with the range and scope of the writer's historical sweep. We are trying to connect the author's personal narrative with the larger human narrative to come (two hundred thousand years of human history, Marlene tells us). Diane reminds us that the statement "All macrohistory is autobiographical" is one of those picket fences designed to keep the rest of us out, with its absolute, "take no prisoners" quality ("All . . .") and its union of the seemingly contradictory terms "macrohistory" and "autobiographical." She implies that the writer has an obligation to be clearer and more accessible from the start, especially in a text designed for uninitiated students. I find Diane's response most interesting in light of her own inside perspective on our earlier piece on diabetes treatments. There she assumed, and understood, the writer's complex motives and rich technical expertise. Now she is on the outside and feels considerable discomfort in that position.

Kathy, whose own expertise is rooted in her ability to navigate the linguistic and cultural styles of her ESL students, observes that the piece poses terrific challenges for all of us in this room, let alone those students who must come to it as uninitiated in the discipline. I ask her and the others if the difficulty arises from its specialized vocabulary or rather from a way of seeing experience. To get at some answers, we look closely at the following:

> . . . the task of appraising those societies and relating them to our times and needs is correspondingly formidable. It becomes more manageable only when it is noted that all of these hundreds of past and present human societies fall into three broad categories: kinship societies, encompassing all human communities until about 2500 BC; tributary societies . . . which appeared first in the Middle East about 3500 BC . . . ; and free-market, or capitalist societies, which first appeared in northwestern Europe about 1500 AD. . . . (11)

What distinguishes such writing, according to Marlene, is the way in which the author takes a massive amount of experience, the countless forms of human societies, and groups them in terms of "basic modes of production" (Marlene's words). He then attempts to draw "lifelines" among the groupings, that is, categories of human experience that run through the groups: "ecology, gender relations, social relations, and war" (11). The writer does not pretend to write an exhaustive history of humanity: "This book is instead a highly selective analysis of those aspects of the past that illuminate our present. It is, in short, an inquiry into our usable past" (12). The challenge for readers outside the writer's area of expertise is to be comfortable with the paradigm constructed. That level of comfort rises or falls depending on our willingness and ability not only to accept these categories as viable but also to draw the "lifelines" between microhistory and macrohistory. The task is formidable for writer and reader.

Kathy, for one, reaches an acceptance of the writer's broad method, based in part on her familiarity with Marlene's perspective: "You want to look from the people up," she says to Marlene. "That's what he was saying, that history is all of our autobiographies." Peter adds a corrective reading by saying, "I think he means autobiography not as a personal thing but autobiography of the human race." These are both astute readings. Taken together they represent the challenge of the writer's task: to render history as a human story.

To make this lesson explicit, Marlene shares an assignment with us from her early modern European history course. In that assignment, which is the first of the course, she asks her students to consider the question, "Was there a Renaissance for women?" Implicit in that question, of course, is a rereading of the Renaissance to include multiple stories, multiple perspectives on that historical period. (How, in other words, did the Renaissance affect a wide range of society—not simply powerful men?)

Even more interesting to me is the glimpse that Marlene's assignment provides of historical methods:

> Like many historians, you are confronted with evidence that might seem contradictory, uneven, and fragmentary. Your task is to make sense of this by analyzing the evidence, trying to spot patterns, overarching themes, and/or inconsistencies, and then drawing some conclusions.
>
> *There is no right or wrong answer to this question!*

As I look back at this assignment, I am fascinated by Marlene's use of that term "evidence." In the current version of our list of "primary traits" of good writing, evidence is simply said to be the detail that writers use to persuade readers. The assumption is that, with the proper use of evidence, clarity and truth can be achieved. Marlene, however, asks us (and her students) to view "evidence" as sometimes yielding contradiction and incompleteness. She is clearly bringing a distinct set of expectations to that term, reflecting a social epistemic that our "primary traits" do not. In asking her students to write "like many historians," Marlene wants them to sift through many perspectives and stories and to establish an interpretation that, for the time, brings order to the many "inconsistencies" that history can offer. That interpretation, like the "normal" science that Thomas Kuhn describes, may itself be challenged and overturned by a competing and ultimately more credible interpretation (1962, 10). I cannot help adding, however, that in going so far as saying, "There is no right or wrong answer to this question," Marlene undermines the premise of her assignment. All interpretations are not equal. To make the claim that truths, historical or otherwise, are socially constructed (reflecting the inherently limited perspectives of human beings), should not open the door to outright relativism. "Right answers" are indeed achievable; beliefs can acquire the authority of consensus and convention. Paraphrasing the words of the historian R. H. Tawney that begin the "Lifelines" piece, Marlene observes, "Every generation has to reinvent history," taking from it what that generation needs. The interpretation that emerges has currency and legitimacy.

All this talk about "using history" brings us back, of course, to those students whose view of historical writing is that it is disconnected from their own worlds. How do we enable them to draw their own "lifelines" to history? "Would you allow your students," I ask Marlene, "to become more autobiographical in their own writing" so as to begin to "use" history? But in asking that question I fall into the trap of confusing individual and personal autobiography with the "autobiography of the human race," as Peter puts it. The point is not to tell their own stories, but rather to see history as encompassing a multiplicity of stories. We run a similar risk in writing courses when we privilege individual students' stories rather than have students work with a range of experiences offered in texts written by nonstudents. To write from experience ought not to be narrowly circumscribed by students' own "voices" and private autobiographies but should include a host of voices and a convergence of narratives. Perhaps the kind of writing that we ought to be considering in our courses is what Mary Louise Pratt calls "autoethnography," in which writers represent themselves "in dialogue" with other stories, other representations (1992, 7). Autoethnographic texts, as Pratt defines them, are written by "others" or outsiders involving "collaboration with and appropriation of the idioms of the conqueror" (7). In terms of the classroom, students may write autoethnographic pieces as a way to respond to the powerful and authoritative stories of their teachers and their assigned reading (Bartholomae 1993). In any event, the goal becomes not to write merely personal stories, nor simply to mimic teachers and texts. Rather, it is a way for students to "use" their subjects and to become immersed in them.

Such writing invariably requires struggle because writers must work with and through authoritative accounts to tell their own stories. Indeed, the historian whose writing we have been discussing may be struggling himself to draw the "lifelines" of history. Marlene, speaking of her own students, admits that she wants them to struggle in "using" history. She wants them to reinvent history in light of their own needs.

Kathy, as is so often the case, redirects us to the practical needs of our students. She asks whether our particular students, students who come to the community college with a wide array of backgrounds and levels of preparedness, are ready to engage in such a struggle, to wrestle with a difficult text as we have done here. Diane voices her agreement and wonders whether such writing might intimidate less confident readers and writers. Wouldn't it make more sense to have students read pieces "written by classmates down more to their level, [so] that they would understand and be less intimidated by it?"

"Down more to their level"—taken out of context these words might suggest a condescension toward our students, a feeling that they cannot handle difficult readings, and that we need to "dumb down" our instruction and our reading lists in order to teach them. Diane does not mean that. Rather, like Kathy, she brings to our discussion a set of assumptions about this college's mission that need to be recognized. They emphasize what our college catalog calls a "learner-centered environment," in which the students' varied needs are taken into account. They also remind us of the comprehensive nature of our college, whose purpose seems broader than to train future historians.

But the issues raised here are not cut and dried, of course. We are all trained academics, hired to share our experience and expertise in the academy with our students. Marlene, in asking her students to struggle with and "reinvent history," is hardly ignoring her students' needs. In fact, she wants her students to "relate" to what she teaches but, in her own words, "You want to move people beyond that" [too]. She wants her students to listen to and grasp stories other than their own.

A similar discussion has been played out in composition studies for years. When Mina Shaughnessy demonstrated that the work of basic writing students deserved the kind of close reading that the academy reserved for cherished canonical texts, she sent out the message that student texts ought to be central in our courses (1977). The same can be said for Peter Elbow, whose concern over the years has been to show that student writing must have pride of place in any supportive writing community (1973; 1981). Within the last decade, however, other perspectives on student work have emerged. David Bartholomae has issued a call that writing students— including basic writers—be immersed in the work of the academy, not simply to conform to it but rather to discover or "invent" the university for themselves (1986). Others, like Min-Zhan Lu, have challenged Shaughnessy's view of the basic writing classroom as discrete and insular and have advocated using that classroom as a setting for the study of cultural texts, not to be limited to the students' work alone (1991; 1992).

The mission of the community college, with its broad and comprehensive purpose to train a thoughtful citizenry, would seem to place it outside this "academic" debate. But, in fact, as we have seen, it is at the community college that the debate is put into its sharpest relief. With a student body roughly split between those who intend to transfer to four-year institutions and those who plan to go directly to the workplace, and with a faculty whose background reflects both academic training and workplace experience, the community college cannot afford to ignore the critical question, What kind of knowledge do we want our students to leave us with? Put in the terms that Marlene must face every day in her classroom, the questions might be, Am I endowing my students with insights into historical methods? or, Am I providing them with more generalizable skills, appropriate for the workplace? Put more profoundly, our question might very well go to the nature of general education itself: What kind of persons do we want our students to become?

5 Responding to Student Writing

I want to set up a situation where [I] avoid conflict. . . . The goal is to reply to an assignment, keeping in sight that it's a combined effort, that the teacher is a facilitator, not the originator of the work.

—Pat

It's wrong if you don't tell him the truth.

—Marlene

Before becoming part of our college's writing lab, all of us, of course, have had plenty of experience responding to student writing. But the experience of tutoring students in the lab has forced us to reexamine our ways of reading and responding to student work. In large part, that has occurred because our reading of those papers is no longer tied to giving a grade; as tutors we have far less vested in the writing. Our comments, whether written or presented orally, are meant to motivate and guide revision, not justify an assessment. We respond in order to facilitate students' efforts to improve their writing.

Inevitably, our lab experience, then, has prompted us to ask, How do we currently respond to the writing of our own students? If our responses do not produce the outcomes that we want, how can we change the way we write and talk back to our students' writing? Responding to student writing is a curious business, to say the least. We spend much time and effort on responding to student work and yet we have little opportunity to reflect on exactly what it is we are doing. What is our purpose in responding? Is it to allow students to return to their work with a clearer sense of what must be done? If so, why do our comments so often serve as a gloss of (or justification for) our grading, rather than an invitation to revise? In many courses, says Debbie, a student tutor in the lab, "there's no room for revision." What kind of motivation is there for students to read and use teachers' comments?

What exactly is happening when students read our comments, anyway? Kathy tells a revealing story of some of her ESL students, who, in "revising" their papers, "included my correcting comments as if they belonged to the text." In some ways, their "mimicking" of the teacher is not so far removed from native speakers' ways of reading teachers' commentary. Our writing does "belong" to the text as codes of acceptable writing conduct, and students know what it will take to get that A (or F) on the basis of the teacher's commentary. The fact that teachers might very well see their comments as "correcting" as well of course fuels the belief that the writing is the teacher's anyway—so why not give teachers what they want?

Marlene claims to have a different problem: her students sometimes ignore her comments entirely in their revision. "I couldn't understand that," she says. What prevents our students from "getting" what we are saying? Is it a matter of the tone we assume as teacher commentators? Do we turn students off with our exasperated comments? Do we cut corners, rubber-stamp our remarks, in light of the sheer load of papers that we have to grade? Jerry reminds us that a teacher "may have thirty other papers" to grade (composition teachers might double or triple that number). "It is difficult," he says, "to find time to do justice to the writer." Diane notes the wear and tear of reading so many papers with the same kind of error: "The repetitiveness of the errors deadens sensitivity." More fundamentally, however, perhaps our difficulty has something to do with a set of assumptions that we bring to students' work: assumptions about the right way to do an assignment and assumptions about our own authority as readers.

To get at some insights into the process of reading and responding to student work, our group read two pieces that highlight research done on teacher response: one by Nancy Sommers (1982), the other by Lil Brannon and C. H. Knoblauch (1984). Sommers's research, done in collaboration with Brannon and Knoblauch, yields the following findings:

- teachers' comments often divert students from their own purposes in writing to a focus on the teachers' purposes;

- teachers' comments are often not specific to the students' text but "could be interchanged, rubber-stamped, from text to text" (Sommers 1982, 149, 152).

As an example of the first finding, Sommers reproduces a paragraph from a student's essay, together with the teacher's marginal and interlinear comments. She notes the "contradictory messages" reflected in the teacher's remarks ("Wordy—be precise"; "This paragraph needs to be expanded"), which set up expectations on the one hand for mere editing changes, and, on the other hand, for more significant ones, including fuller development of ideas (150).

Sommers's findings paint a dismal portrait of the way teachers read and respond to their students' work. Are we really so unreflective and unsympathetic in our reading of student essays? Much of what Sommers has to say strikes a chord with us. Diane, referring to an example of teacher commentary that seems generic or "rubber-stamped," agrees that the teacher's comments as given are less than helpful: "'Be specific' means nothing. It's better to ask a direct question: 'What technology are you referring to?'"

In this particular paper (on nuclear power), the teacher needs to engage the content as well as the form, needs to talk about the seeming contradiction in the point of view. Marlene seems genuinely taken by what Sommers has to say, admitting, painfully, that "all the stuff I have been writing is useless." She sees the need to be "more specific" herself in her commentary, the need to engage the students' words and ideas directly. As I hear Marlene say this, however, I think of those times when we are "specific" and extensive in our feedback and, still, students don't quite seem to "get it." Something else, clearly, is going on in those cases. Very likely, the grades that usually accompany our commentaries shade our students' responses. I share with the group my experiment some years ago with eliminating the grading of drafts in my composition courses. That change seemed to liberate me in ways I could not have anticipated. Students now read my responses with the intention of using them to produce stronger drafts. And I don't have to agonize over whether to give a B- or a C+. Rather I can focus on facilitating students' work through the most precise feedback that I can muster.

Pat raises the ante by asking, "How do we handle the challenge of a student paper that has a wide range of problems?" She tells about the challenge of reading one such paper:

> [My students] hand me about eight papers a semester. There's a lot of writing, and a lot of reading for me, and a lot of comments that I give back. . . .This [student's] paper was unreadable. I waited two hours and said it must be me, I must be tired. I'll get back to it. Over four days I read that paper ten times. And I could not make any sense out of that paper. It did not flow. It was stilted. The language was absolutely unbelievable. Sentences went on and on. It was beyond me.

Her comments ranged from "We need to go over this" to "Your sentences are too long." Kathy rightly reminds the group that such problems fall under editing skills rather than revision. She echoes Sommers's concern that we teachers not confuse the two. The difference between the two, Sommers observes, is the difference between seeing the student text as essentially fixed and seeing it as evolving (151). Too often students come to our paper conferences or to our writing lab with the first notion in mind: that all that needs to be done is "clean up" the grammar. In confusing editing with revision, we at best reinforce that idea and at worst thoroughly confuse and stymie the student writer.

But to return to the scenario posed by Pat: How do we respond to a paper gone badly wrong, reflecting a whole host of problems? What do we do when, as Peter witnessed recently in the writing lab, the writing is "atrocious, full of affectation, posing, lies, dishonesty," and the writer "can barely string together some sentences?" Of course, as Marlene reminds us, we have to "tell him the truth." But we need as well to provide what Ann Berthoff calls "assisted invitations" (1978, 2): a way of reseeing the text and a motivation to struggle further with it. Our feedback must reside in language that is supportive, truthful, immediate, and without "handbook jargon" (the notorious "awk" or "frag").

Peter offers the view that we can lessen the pressure on our written comments on student writing by achieving an appropriate level of response within our classrooms, that is, by using the classroom to demonstrate a "good critical stance." Early on in his writing courses, he hands out a sheet spelling out such a stance and talks about it. He also brings in "all kinds of good writing" to test out students' responses. Throughout all of this, Peter's students are reading their papers to the class regularly, giving and getting critical feedback.

In creating such an atmosphere of supportive yet frank discussion of student work, Peter goes a long way toward defusing some of the issues that we are discussing: less stress is placed on the teacher's written feedback, since students are also getting feedback from other sources (one another) on a continual basis; and the teacher's mode of response is enacted and demonstrated in class throughout the semester.

It seems that in the process laid out here Peter is shaping his students' responses from the beginning (starting with the handout he mentions): they take their cue from him. More interesting to me would be a process of negotiation wherein students and teacher together enact a mode of response. Doing so would require from teachers a jettisoning of what Brannon and Knoblauch call the "inappropriate tyranny of an Ideal Text" (1984, 121). Teachers must read students' work without imposing on it, as Carol puts it, a "preconceived paper." Students, as all writers do, must attend to readers' expectations, most especially the teachers'.

Too often such negotiation is seen reductively, that is, as a selling out either by student or by the teacher. In fact, one of our peer tutors, Bob, who is an older returning student at our community college, wonders why he would have to "change [his] writing when [he goes] from teacher to teacher." "I write," he says, "my own way." Kathy, recognizing Bob's legitimate concerns, attempts to distinguish between a writer's "person" and the form and purpose of the writing:

> Your person has to come through in whatever you write. And no teacher should try to take that away. But the assignment can change the thrust of how you write. . . . If [Marlene] sets up an assignment asking you to write to the King and Queen of Spain that's a different kind of writing from how you feel about the birth of your daughter.

Bob fears the loss of control over his writing, understandably, given his reading of the negotiation between writer and reader. It doesn't help matters that Peter, a published writer, reveals that he sees readers (most especially magazine and book editors) as "obstacles . . . to overcome." Peter tells a story of his own dogged efforts to "overcome" the obstacle of a particular reader:

> I've been writing short stories since last summer. [The editor of a magazine] has rejected six in a row. . . . Finally, he told me what he wanted. What he wanted was a story with a comic curve. An old, traditional story with a comic curve. And I realized all of a sudden that this is what he wants. Guess what I'm writing? A story with a comic curve.

We may legitimately ask who is overcoming whom here when Peter must adjust to the formal expectations of his editor in order to get published in a particular magazine. Bob may very well see Peter's story as an example of excessive compromise. But Peter assures us that he has not lost control of his writing in the process of adjusting to his editor's expectations. Within the expansive form in which he is expected to write, he can write the way that he wishes. The fact is, of course, Peter strikes a compromise, in the appropriate sense of the word. Intent on being published in a particular magazine, he is realistic enough to know that he must give as well as take. He strikes a balance between the needs of his reader and his own needs as a writer. In doing so, Peter demonstrates a level of maturity and experience that Bob will have to reach if he wishes to write for others.

Peter's story raises an issue larger than how to write for readers. It speaks to the degree to which any of us wields control over decisions that affect us. I am reminded of this larger theme when I hear Diane speak of the relevance of our discussion of authorship and authority to her own field of nursing:

> In nursing we call that the locus of decision, meaning who has the right to make the decision. There are times when the locus of decision is the patient. If you make the decision not to have chemotherapy, I may disagree with you but that's not my decision. My responsibility is to support you. . . . So with editors, is the locus of decision mine? or his? It's nicest if it's both.

That last observation is terribly important since it avoids a naive reading of the "locus" of authority. Certainly patients have, ultimately, the "right" to make decisions affecting their health and welfare. But those decisions may very likely come after an exchange of views among all parties. Moreover, patients (and students) do not "make decisions" innocent of institutional pressures—the hospital and the school are obviously very much alike in the unequal distribution of authority between doctor and patient (or doctor and nurse) and teacher and student. Patients face enormous pressures to defer to attending doctors when it comes to "what is right" for them, just as students may have to think long and hard before challenging the authority of their teachers.

If we teachers accept the view (as Sommers, Brannon, and Knoblauch apparently do) that the "locus of decision" ought to be the students, how do we put aside the authority that our institutions expect us to have? Diane puts the question in more concrete and dramatic terms: What do we do as teachers when students challenge our cherished beliefs in their writing? Indeed, the way we read student work differs, she argues, depending on the stake that we teachers have in the ideas expressed. We will read more critically if the position taken runs counter to our beliefs. Generally, she says, "it's very difficult to be objective" under those circumstances.

Peter, for his part, will have nothing to do with the straitjacket that Diane would put him and the rest of us in. "When I read a paper and disagree with everything that is being said," Peter observes, "I honestly try not to be prejudiced." That admission may in fact support Diane's point—that we cannot escape the authority of our position. In this case, Peter must work to "try not to be prejudiced." All papers are not read the same way: Peter must adjust his way of reading when it comes to those papers that challenge his perspectives.

Is there a way, as Marlene suggests, of "letting go of some of that power" that teachers inevitably possess? Can we read and respond to student work in a genuinely facilitative way (rather than in a merely peremptory, directive fashion), allowing students to maintain ownership over their writing? Can we set up conditions so that the "locus of decision" is indeed the student? As a way to get at some answers, we look closely at an illustration given in the Brannon and Knoblauch piece. The authors reproduce a student essay, in draft and in final form, together with comments from the teacher and the student writer. The earlier version of the essay attempts to link smoking—in particular the annoying smoking habit of a roommate—with a decline in morality ("There are no morals left in this world . . . . Unfortunately I live with this example [of immorality] everyday. It is my roommate" [133]). The connection between the decline in morality and the roommate's habit of smoking is not persuasively made at all.

The teacher's comments on this earlier draft point out this rhetorical and logical problem but seem to do so in a fairly tactful and facilitative way, summarizing the student's argument and proceeding to ask probing questions:

> You seem to be saying that there's no more morality left in the world. You exemplify your belief with reference to your roommate's smoking. You seem to be puzzled about why anyone would pick up this immoral habit and thrust it upon innocent victims like yourself. . . .
> My central question is why do you link smoking with morality? Is smoking really a misdeed equivalent to illicit sex and cheating? Is

smoking as terrible as stealing? If so, would you explain why? I have
known some kind and generous people who happened to smoke.
Should I consider them to be as terrible as rapists and wife-beaters?
. . . (134)

Upon handing in the revision, the student responds to the teacher's feedback (and to a peer's reading of the same paper) in this way:

> Thank you for your comments on my draft. Your comments combined
> with my group's were helpful. Pamela's reaction to my paper was un-
> expected. She thought that my emotions were overriding the theme
> of the work. . . .
>
> But your reactions to my paper, *defensive as they were*, proved to me
> that it is impossible to divorce emotion from content. Now that I have
> finished the paper I believe it has lost some of the brimstone that I
> originally intended. . . .
>
> Otherwise, any issue as to whether it is morally right or not, is
> beyond the intent of my paper and not within my grasp at this point.
> . . . (135; italics mine)

As the writer reveals, the new version of the paper leaves aside the theme
of moral decline, focusing on the difficulties of dealing with a roommate
who smokes. The paper shows considerably more control than the earlier draft.

Our discussion of the teacher's role in the revision draws unexpected
responses. On the one hand, the teacher strikes us as being supportive,
and very far from assertive and directive. Kathy's take is representative of
what many of us feel: "The teacher questions the thesis whether smoking
is a moral issue and asks him to rethink that. The student was free to come
back and make a case that smoking is a moral issue. You could have made
a case." Marlene concurs by saying that the teacher tactfully demonstrates
a flaw in the student's reasoning: "You cannot compare smoking with
rape." The fact that at least one of the writer's peer reviewers sees an ex-
cess of emotion seems to support the teacher's claims.

But some of us, notably Pat and Diane, read the teacher's comments
as subtly coercive. Indeed Pat infers that the teacher is a smoker and "was
offended by the linking" of smoking and immorality. The student's own
astute comments about the teacher's defensiveness seem to be saying that
the teacher has some vested interest in the subject. The language used by
the teacher would suggest as much, heavily freighted as it is with emotion
("rape", "wife-beaters"). Diane wonders whether the seemingly facilitative
questions really reveal the teacher's own agenda: jettison the morality
theme altogether or suffer the consequences. "If you were really the ideal
[facilitator]," Diane observes, "you would encourage the student to develop the morality theme." It is a shrewd observation, to say the least. The
teacher ought to have entered into the student's argument and stayed

there, offering suggestions that would enable the student to make it convincingly. In other words, the teacher is really not able to engage the student's position imaginatively (to play what Peter Elbow calls the "believing game" [1986, 25]). Perhaps the best evidence of the problematic nature of the teacher's feedback is the revised essay itself. Certainly more reasonable, the piece, however, has lost its edge, its heart ("Moving away to school in a new city can involve many dramatic and new situations," begins the new version [135]). It may very well be true, as Kathy suggests, that the student changes the essay more in response to peer pressure than to teacherly authority, and the importance of such mediating voices cannot be overstated. Nevertheless we cannot but see this paper slipping away from the student.

Can we as teachers provide genuinely facilitative responses to our students' writing? We all believe it can happen, although it requires an acknowledgment of our own prejudices and predispositions. The teacher whose remarks we have been studying may very well have played the facilitative role, given that teacher's knowledge of the student's capabilities and the scope of the assignment (context which is not given in the researchers' account). What is missing, however, is an awareness of the teacher's own implicit position.

Reducing our reliance on an "Ideal Text" may also go a long way toward making us more sympathetic readers of students' work. As we design assignments, we ought to phrase questions or set tasks that have, as Diane says, a "possibility of more than one answer." The difficulty of doing so becomes all too clear when Jerry, on my request, shares an assignment of his own from his introductory statistics course, along with some student samples (and his marginal comments on them). The assignment asks for a comparison of two populations in order "to show the inappropriate comparison being made":

> The death rate of Navy personnel during the Spanish American War was nine per thousand. At the same time in New York City, the death rate of the civilian population was sixteen per thousand. Navy recruiters later used these figures to show that it was safer to be in the Navy than out of it. Assume these figures to be accurate. Show that the figures, as used by the recruiters, are virtually meaningless.

In setting the assignment, Jerry clearly wants his students to learn, as he tells us, "to distrust statistics." He wants them to think critically before accepting such arguments. The difficulty that many of us have with the assignment—most notably Marlene and Diane—is that Jerry leaves his students with little opportunity to make their writing their own. There is but one answer—or a set of answers—which guides the students in their writing and the teacher in his responses to it. Inevitably, students then must embark on discovering "what the teacher wants," and the teacher must comment on students' responses in light of a "preconceived text." In his marginal comments, Jerry does play the facilitator, asking questions and referring to what students are actually writing ("Age is a factor—but why?"), but he and the students are virtually "on the same page." It should also be noted that because students were not given the option to revise, Jerry's comments could not facilitate improvement in a particular essay.

To reflect on our own language of critique, we read closely one student's essay on the problem. Considered a relatively competent piece by Jerry (the writer showing reasons to "distrust" the numbers), the essay begins tentatively and informally before moving on to provide useful evidence to repudiate the comparison. For Peter, however, the tentative opening reveals a problem of style that he claims mars the piece from beginning to end. The essay begins in this way:

> It pleases me that the fact has been acknowledged that the comparison is very inappropriate. It is inappropriate because the groups of people being compared have few, if any, similarities. It is similar, however, to comparing apples and oranges.

The paragraph says very little. Peter is struck by the "nervous" tone. The student does not know where to begin, and so adopts a pseudosophisticated style (what Ken Macrorie years ago called "Engfish" [1970, 18]).

The next paragraph sees the student adopt a far less formal stance:

> What's frightening is that before taking this course I might not have realized such a statement to be inaccurate, at least not as quickly. I think the reason for this is that previously, I had such a negative feeling about numbers. . . . Consequently, I always took statements like this for truth without every giving any thought. It is unfortunate that many young men may have signed up with a recruiter based solely on this pitch.

For Peter, this paragraph is simply proof that the writer has little control over language or material ("He's been very formal all along and ends with 'this pitch'"). The conclusion (which begins tritely with "All things considered . . ." and ends with the bland assertion "The Navy is using two populations with completely different variables") is as ineffective as the opening. Peter ends by saying, "If you're asking for a more effective conclusion, you're asking him to be a more effective thinker . . . more sensitive to his audience . . . more considerate of his material."

Diane, for her part, sees much to like in the work. She likes the self-reflection and frankness of the second paragraph. "It may be worth taking the course just to understand yourself," she claims. As to the rest of the essay, she approves of the evidence brought to bear to support the writer's point ("They were useful facts"), especially a point about the "social unrest" possible in the civilian group. Like Peter, she believes the ending simply is not up to the task but responds that it "might be helpful to list or summarize the variables." She concludes by saying to the student directly, "[You] had a good grasp of the concepts and variables and demonstrate how they were not used in the comparing of the two populations."

In Peter's and Diane's responses, we see two readers each of whom seems to be applying a different set of criteria (their criteria in turn differing from Jerry's). Peter evaluates the piece in terms of its style, which Peter defines as not merely grammar but "word choice, diction, sentence structure . . . the voice of the speaker." Diane, on the other hand, seems closer to engaging the writing on its own terms (hence the admiration for the seemingly "off-topic" second paragraph), although, in expecting the paper to conclude with a summary of what has been said, she sends a signal to the student that essays must have a certain form, at least in terms of the way they must close.

Faced with readers whose critique of their writing may range as widely as those we have just seen, writers must come to see composing as in large part a matter of negotiation between or among competing claims. Perhaps it is best to say that "the locus of decision" rests not in any particular site, but rather at the borders across which such negotiation takes place.

6 Is All Knowledge Provisional?

Would you rather have heard Lincoln's Gettysburg Address or would it be better sitting in your room quietly reading it?

—Diane

When we approach a piece of writing with what Lil Brannon and C. H. Knoblauch call an Ideal Text in mind, the writing becomes little more than a reflective surface, giving us a version of our ourselves. If we wish to view writing as creative and meaningful, then as readers we need to view it, and the writers who produce it, with very different expectations. Reading ought in part to be an act of discovery. Moreover, we ought to view students' work as worthy of our exploration. "Students come in with frames of reference, sets of ideas, whole structures in their minds," says Marlene. They do not come to us "vacant." Of course, to deny that we readers help shape that "structure" and give meaning to the text is to lose sight of the complex negotiation that takes place between readers and writers.

Our discussion of that negotiation takes on a more philosophical dimension when Marlene discusses her work on critical thinking. Specifically, she has found it useful to approach a piece of writing by asking questions like the following, each of which implies an "element of reasoning":

- What is the purpose?
- What is the point of view or frame of reference of the writer?
- What is the evidence that supports the argument?
- What are the assumptions underlying the argument?

Behind the critical thinking approach, she says, is the fact that "every single piece of reasoning has these different elements. . . . An object to be figured out, some data, some experience of it; some reason for wanting to figure it out; some question we want solved." Granted that each discipline carries its own "logic," there must be, she claims, a common, universal framework to that logic. At the heart of the "elements" is the belief that all objects have "something to figure out." In fact, all objects have "a logic." Peter is quick to seize upon that point:

> You say a discipline has a logic, but here [on Marlene's handout] it says an object has a logic. I find it interesting because it is a kind of William James concept, a reciprocity between the knowing mind and the object known. There is in fact an internal logic to the object, that

44

the knowing mind somehow needs to discover. . . . He's discovering, not creating.

Peter goes on to draw a connection to the romantic view, whereby nature has inherent meaning—which can be reflected or illuminated by the knowing mind. It is interesting that Peter moves from recognizing the reciprocity between the knowing mind and the object known to emphasizing the meaning inherent in the object itself.

What drives Peter to highlight that fact is the "act of faith" implicit in it: we can come upon the truth of things. Moreover, as Marlene adds, not only is the object knowable "but *I* can know it." Our students too can know it. For Marlene, as well as Peter, such a notion carries with it a refreshing optimism. As community college teachers, we are likely to be motivated by the belief that our students can, given the opportunity, get to a workable set of "truths."

It is ironic, then, that Marlene is the one who seems to undermine that very optimism. All along in these discussions she has talked about the importance of historical perspective and of history as an artifact, a construct of interpretations. Now she goes further to say, "This framework [that is, the "Elements of Reasoning"] shows how relativistic the truth is, that everyone's got a point of view, that you have to look deeper and see where arguments lead." In saying so, Marlene is actually following up on something that Chris has said earlier:

> Richard Paul [a proponent of critical thinking] makes a mistake when he says there's an object to be figured out at the start. That is open to discussion. The [view] in the twentieth century is that we construct the argument.

Marlene and Chris's view of knowledge does not sit well with Peter, who, on hearing Marlene use the term "relativistic," again speaks passionately about knowing as an "act of faith":

> Don't we have to have a faith in knowing? Don't we have to say that we both discover and create? If we assume that we create entirely, then there is no possibility of achieving anything except what's in your own consciousness. You have to posit an external truth. Otherwise everything else floats in your own consciousness.

Those who hold to the view that knowledge is socially constructed do not, of course, deny external or material truths. In fact, scholars who have posited a view of knowledge as provisional—Richard Rorty, for one, comes to mind—may be seen as following an established American tradition of pragmatism (West 1989). It is useful to believe that truths are formed by and within human communities, supported or rejected by members of such communities. Such notions, when accepted, then become part of the "normal" (in Kuhn's sense of the word) thinking of that community, guiding its members from day to day (Kuhn 1962). Everyone indeed may have an opinion on a matter but opinions gain currency only when a consensus builds around them, a consensus tested and supported by the authority of the best available evidence.

While Peter may be confusing a consensus view of knowledge with a relativistic view, he is right to voice concern about "breaking faith" in our confidence in our capacity to get to the truth. Diane reminds us of this point when she speaks about the peculiar situation confronting our students:

> . . . our students are in a society that alienates them from reading and writing. They don't write letters; they use the phone. They don't take minutes at a meeting; they use a tape recorder. They don't read a newspaper; they listen to the TV or radio. . . . It's not unusual for people to say [they've] never read a novel.

The "alienation" that Diane speaks of is from a stable, authoritative form of truth, for that is what the conventionally printed text has provided. Of course, Diane does not mention the writing that students *are* doing: through e-mail, chat programs, list servers, to mention just a few stations on the information highway (Faigley 1992). Electronic communication—most spectacularly, through computer networks—has rendered the written text less permanent, less reliable than ever before.

In light of these changes, Peter raises a related question: "How do you defend reading and writing?" Diane seconds Peter's question by asking, "Why write instead of talking into a tape?" It is true that all of us sitting in this room are committed to teaching reading and writing in their conventional senses. All of us know the good that can come from these activities. But, having said that, I take these questions not as mere "devil's advocacy." As committed as we all are to the conventional processes of reading and writing, perhaps we all feel the need to recognize the changing nature of literacy in the last years of the twentieth century.

"Why write?" Given who we are, the question might seem heretical. Yet it is clearly important that we ask it and try to answer it. If nothing else, the challenge posed by nonprint media forces us to consider closely what happens when we write, a process that we rarely reflect upon. Peter, for his part, responds to the question "Why write?" by becoming philosophical: "[Writing] allows us to develop or create for ourselves a means of accessing part of our nature and part of the world. Otherwise they remain inaccessible." Seeing writing as a means to access "part of the world," Peter seems to echo Paulo Freire and Donaldo Macedo's notion that in writing the word we write the world as well (1987). It is true that for Freire and Macedo writing is transformative, a means of changing conditions in the world, whereas Peter speaks only of "accessing" the world. But in an institution—such as a community college—where access leads students to gain power over their lives, Peter's view of writing has as much trans-formative power as in Freire and Macedo's view.

Moreover, if access to the world leads to transformation of that world, then having access to "part of our nature" might have a similar effect on our own consciousness. Peter notes this phenomenon when he says, "The advance in human consciousness occurred when somebody put down a symbol and somebody knew what it meant." Rather than view writing as merely a technological innovation, Peter, like Walter Ong, sees writing as altering fundamentally our sense of ourselves (Ong 1982). After all, when that symbol became understood by another, the writer's consciousness expanded to include that other.

Jerry reminds us that, when we write, the whole person comes into play: "Your mind, your emotion, your vision, your physical [nature]." Writing is then truly "composing," a bringing together of disparate parts. It be-comes, in Wordsworth's terms, a means of joining thought and feeling, of recollecting emotion in tranquility. Wordsworth reminds us of the power of writing to offer a deepening perspective on the fleeting moment, and I am thinking of that notion during an exchange between Diane and Chris. Diane, in considering the differences between reading a written text and listening to a spoken performance of that text, asks, "Would you rather have *heard* Lincoln's Gettysburg Address or would it be better sitting in your room quietly reading it?" Her question implies a privileging of the speech as it was given—who wouldn't want to have been present at that momentous occasion? But Chris refuses to take the bait. He notes that the speech when delivered had little effect on the immediate audience (in fact Lincoln may have had the audience of posterity in mind). "It was only through the historical perspective [provided through] reading," he adds, that the power of the speech was felt.

Chris goes on to say that writing provides a form of argument that vi-sual media cannot: the argument implied in subordination of clauses and sentences, for example. Moreover, a written text, Diane reminds us, lends itself to analysis more readily than a spoken performance. And it offers the opportunity of revision, of a second chance.

At this point, Kathy takes issue with our assumptions about the nature of reading and writing. She recently worked with a blind ESL student for whom writing and reading would seem to be quite different from our conventional views. "Legally," she says, such students "write if they can compose." They may have a scribe who writes down what they dictate. Kathy found herself in the position of allowing a student to complete a writing course without writing, as it were.

And yet all these complications and philosophical points aside, each of us—especially at the community college—will have students who wonder why we are asking them to write in our courses. It is a legitimate question for all kinds of reasons, not the least of which is the real possibility that few of them will write when they leave the classroom. And even if employers do ask them to write, is our response simply the utilitarian one?

When I ask Jerry why he has his students write in his statistics course, he can hardly rely upon a functional response (students most definitely will not learn to write memos in his course). Instead, Jerry speaks of writing as a "mental exercise" and as a "record" of their thinking. Judging from the assignment on comparing populations, we might also infer that for Jerry writing offers students an opportunity to interrogate arguments and claims made in the world outside the classroom.

For Pat, writing in dental hygiene has two purposes: integration of material and assessment of students' clinical and course performance. Through writing, students come to see the connectedness of what they are learning. They are able to connect classroom reading and lecture material with problems that they encounter in their clinical work. And they are assessed on the basis of their written accounts of that work.

Diane, whose nursing students write up rather detailed care plans for their patients, admits that the question—Why write?—is one that she wrestles with. "Why do we put ourselves through reading these care plans every week?" she asks. The patient care plan requires that the writer detail, in strict sequence and with considerable precision, the treatment given to each patient. The demands of the form on both students and teachers are formidable. She wonders aloud whether a recently developed electronic care plan would make more sense, given the rigors of a nurse's work. Still, in thinking about the peculiar advantages that writing offers, Diane sees the strengths of the care plan as a written document in large part in its humanity:

> You need to treat the person who has that disease. Machines don't do that . . . [Machines] don't worry about the fact that there's nobody home but the five kids. [They] don't worry about the fact that [patients] have been beaten up at home and don't want to go home.

Beyond the detail and precision, writing, for Diane, "treats the person." It is a human and humane technology, a window into the soul of the writer, of the subject, and of the reader.

For Kathy, writing has less to do with expressing one's humanity than with creating opportunities for students to become clear thinkers. When

I hear Kathy say this, I wonder whether, in asking ESL students to write in English, Kathy asks more of them than to be clear. Is she not asking them, in fact, to familiarize themselves with, and adapt to, our culture? Interestingly, Kathy construes my use of the word "culture" to refer to that of the academy: "As a teacher of ESL students and as part of the community college, my responsibility is to help them enter the academic community."

Whether it indeed be adapting to the culture of the academy or to the broader culture of English speakers, writing for these students becomes a powerful tool of assimilation. Perhaps these are the students referred to when Peter says that writing "creates a new consciousness" or when Chris says that by writing "you become."

7 Is Assessing Writing Possible?

What does [personal narrative] have to do with the writing in history, chemistry, or biology? What is in this paper that is transferable?

—Howard

The time has finally arrived to decide whether or not to rework our "criteria for good writing." Given all that we have said (explicitly and implicitly) about discipline-specific ways of knowing, can we assume that our list of primary traits applies to all writing regardless of the discipline? If writing does indeed express the way a discipline "thinks," and if each discipline's thinking does vary in important ways, must we not fashion an evaluative instrument that reflects those differences? Diane, whose instincts as we have seen are to remove the "picket fences" separating disciplines, wonders whether these differences are merely "accidents." The traits that we have recognized (perspective, audience, evidence, logic, correctness) reflect universal principles, she says. I suggest that universal principles may apply even as individual disciplines employ their own methods of inquiry and reporting. Those principles may apply to writing nursing care plans, for example. But care plans may, at the same time, reveal distinctive methods, designs, and expectations. What methods do nurses use, I ask Diane, when treating, and reporting on the treatment of, patients? "The first step," Diane says, "is assessment":

> That's where you go in and gather data. . . . The second step is analysis, where you analyze the facts and sift through them. And you come up with the third, which is the diagnosis. What [do] you feel is the problem . . . ? What is the implication? What are you going to do about the problem . . . ? Then the final stage is evaluation, where you look at what you did and whether or not it worked, and then you revise.

Marlene, surprised at what she hears, asks, "So you don't start off with the hypothesis?" I know why she asks that question. Marlene assumes that an interpretive hypothesis frames an observation. Diane posits an approach that is data-driven. The nurse figures in the equation as an observer only. That role would seem to conflict with the description of the nurse's job given by Diane earlier: the nurse as patient advocate, as very much a player in the patients' treatment. Nevertheless, the writing of the patient's care plan seems to construct a position for nurses that is far more neutral and detached. However, Diane acknowledges, a nurse

50

> might say why he wrote the things he did; he might credential himself in terms of where he's been, and then he might say why he's collected [data] the way he has. When you read a text of history, I'm not so sure it would be so far afield from that same approach.

The reference to history is in response to Marlene's statement, by way of contrast with writing in nursing, that historians "write out of their own experience, beliefs, and value systems, and . . . can't separate those from what they write."

In an effort to zero in on distinctive traits of writing in a discipline, we return to that excerpt from Marlene's history text. In that excerpt, the writer divides up all of human history into schemes or categories: hunter-gatherer, tributary, and capitalistic societies. Marlene notes that the historian sets up these schemes by "modes of production," a fact which reflects his Marxist framework: "There are historians with different ideologies who would group [societies] in different ways." In other words, historians—like scholars in any discipline—write out of their particular framework. But that framework need not reflect disciplinary bias. Instead it may express that particular individual's way of seeing the world—intellectual categories, as Kathy calls them, necessary to the ordering of that person's perspective. Indeed disciplines may contain a vast array of approaches—to the extent, as Marlene sadly reports of her own situation, that we may have "very little in common" with colleagues in our own departments.

If it is true that disciplines themselves cannot find a common language, then any document that attempts to reduce writing to certain universal qualities or "primary traits" may be just wishful thinking. However, this group, because of its commitment to discovering common ground, is determined to give the traits a chance. Are the qualities that we have designated "primary" indeed useful when reading a piece of writing? In order to get at their usefulness, we decide to apply these traits to a problematic piece of student writing. The piece comes from Peter's composition course, a course our college catalog refers to as "Writing from Experience." A required course for all our students—and the only required course in writing—English 11 is commonly perceived by faculty as the one place in the curriculum where students can obtain training in college writing that will prepare them for coursework down the road. No other course carries the weight of such expectations.

Peter sets up our reading by describing the student writer:

> He was told by high school teachers that he couldn't write, that he'd better learn a trade. . . . Even when he got an A on an earlier paper he didn't believe it was any good. . . . There was a real credibility problem. He didn't believe.

Peter consciously sets up a portrait of the student writer as underdog hero, knowing full well that we will be charmed by the piece. And yet the portrait that he draws rings true—especially as a description of community college students. For these students, seeing is not believing. They have had so little positive reinforcement in school that they often expect to fail (yet again). Also typical is the advice given to "learn a trade," in light of such failure. School is seen as "academic" work, for those able to go on to the universities, and to graduate school. It is not seen as applying to the lived experience of most of our students.

Peter describes the student's assignment:

> The purpose or challenge is [to] re-create for the audience, through the use of language, an experience that he has had. And to come as close as he can giving them that experience, making them feel, think, and react as he did.

"What I told this kid," Peter says, "is you've got to tell the truth—no bullshit." In so saying, he privileges the expression of emotion and sets up the standard of "the truth" as a means by which to evaluate such expression. Finally, in merely asking his students to "re-create" a moment Peter invites narrative, rather than explicit analysis.

I read the paper aloud. It begins in conversational mode, addressing the reader directly, and then quickly sets up the story:

> I don't know how many of you have ever experienced death first-hand, but I am here to tell you that I have. It was two-years ago January, when I worked for a large construction company. Things were slow around the office . . . .

Mixing the rhythms of speech with the intricacies of subordination and parallelism, the narrator entices us to enter the experience while at the same time moving economically to describe a central character in the story:

> Lou was about 55 years old, tall, had grey hair, and was a blast to be around. He lived in Little Compton, in a nice little house with his dog. We were never really close, Lou and me, but we did get along.

The narrator knows enough of the man to reveal that "Lou's whole life was his work; his wife died a few years before and his only daughter lived in Texas."

After not hearing from Lou for two weeks, the narrator pays a visit to his house. It is at this point that the story takes on the quality of a "re-created" experience:

> I got out of my truck, and walked toward the breezeway. I could hear Clyde in the house barking, and figured that Lou would greet me at

the door before I could ring the bell. I opened the screen door and was looking at the wooden door, trying to see what was wrong with it. I pulled on the doorknob to pull the door fully closed. Clyde was still barking, and I reached for the handle again, this time to open the door. I turned the knob and gave the door a nudge with my knee. Just then I felt a brush against my leg as Clyde ran out into the front yard. Before I could even open my mouth, I began to gag. The smell coming from inside the house was one that I couldn't describe. It was horrid, like a mixture of old still air, dogshit, and something ten times worse than limberger cheese.

I yelled for Lou, but there wasn't a sound in the house. I held my breath and covered my mouth with the sleeve of my coat. I walked into the house and saw piles of dogshit and puddles of piss all over the kitchen and parlor floors. I knew then that something was wrong. I started climbing the stairs when I saw an arm hanging off the top step. My heart started pounded, and my breath ceased. I continued up the stairs to find Lou on the floor lying in a puddle that looked like mucus. My body started shaking as my eyes focused on the face of a man I didn't recognize. It was Lou, but his skin was now brownish-green, and it was clinging to his face like a leather glove on a hand.

I stood there staring for what seemed to be an eternity. My head was spinning from the smell and sight. I ran downstairs to call the police and then back outside to throw up.

The coroner's report reveals that Lou had died of a heart attack and had been dead for about a week. It also says that "his fingers and forearms had been chewed on by his dog." The narrator notes that at Lou's funeral, which is attended by only nine people, he doesn't really feel loss at Lou's passing "but I do feel bad that he had to die alone."

I enjoy reading the paper aloud, because I feel myself taken by the rhythms and structure of the piece. It seems to verify what Peter often says, "Good writing is like a dance"—allowing us to luxuriate in the sheer joy of movement. And of course I am moved by its dramatic subject and understated treatment of that subject. Narratives, the psychologist Jerome Bruner tells us, derive much of their power from the linking of the "exceptional and the ordinary" (1990, 47). The writer of this story has rendered death in an altogether unexpected way. Others in the room are genuinely moved by the narrative (one of us has to leave the room because, apparently, it hits too close to home): "This *is* magical," Jerry says, echoing Peter's original comments on the work.

I am troubled by Jerry's reaction and by the respectful silence that the piece elicits from the group. How do we articulate a critical response to a piece that works magic? Is our response to be a matter of "faith," and therefore not translatable or accountable? Put another way, how do we explain to faculty outside this room—say a colleague in chemistry—why this piece is strong? What if she says that, sure, this is good but it has very little in common with the kind of writing that she's having her students do? What does expressive writing have to do with the kind of writing that I expect my students to do? In other words, can we extract from this piece certain qualities that can be seen operating in disciplinary writing, universal and transferable qualities inherent in good writing?

Jerry, taking up the challenge, seizes upon the trait of "audience": "I was the audience. He addressed me right away." Jerry is alluding to the description of audience as given in our original list of primary traits:

> If effective communication is to happen, writing must show some sense of audience and a sense of the "rhetorical situation" (the needs of the audience but also the demands of the form of the writing and the purpose).

Working backward from his own affective response to the piece, Jerry argues that his needs as an audience are addressed because he has been so moved by the writer's words. The more critical response would be to explore the ways by which that effect is achieved: How and where does the writer manipulate language so as to maximize the impact on the audience? Pat talks about the way the writer gradually builds up to the climactic discovery of the body—the barking of the dog, the door slightly ajar.

Marlene observes that the writing "had a ring of truth, it had integrity." Referring in part to the realistic description of bodily decay, Marlene may also be speaking about the narrator's equivocal reaction to Lou's passing ("I don't think about Lou too often . . . "). The narrator's detachment from the scene makes a great deal of sense, as does the lingering vision of Lou's neglected corpse.

Peter singles out the carefully modulated, conversational quality of the writing, and links that explicitly to the writer's voice on the page, "a voice that sounds like a person speaking." For Peter, that is the holy grail: to achieve a level of comfort in writing that approaches the ease and gracefulness of speech. More important, and more disturbingly, Peter ties a writer's voice on the page to the "truth" (". . . tell the truth. No bullshit.") It's a view that I have some difficulty with, on several grounds. First of all, since Bakhtin (1981), many have looked at language as polyphonic, containing many voices. In the student's narrative itself, we can indeed hear many voices: from the hip colloquial "shoot the shit" to the subtly ironic "I didn't really feel a loss as I saw his casket surrounded by flowers and fake grass." Any view of a unitary voice would, in addition, seem to contradict the postmodern notion that the self is complex and comprises many selves.

Beyond these broad philosophical concerns, I am struck by Peter's insistence that a piece of writing express the "truth." When I ask Peter what are the qualities in his student's narrative that might transfer to other kinds of writing, his response is quite telling—"voice and personality"— to which I counter: "Are they the same thing?" More than committing the "pathetic fallacy," Peter engages in an ongoing act of faith, a disposition to be charmed by the magic of words. In sharp contrast, I would regard a text as a performance. By that I don't mean to diminish the power of words to move us. Rather I would acknowledge that such power is the outcome of a masterful performance. I am reminded of a question that students seem to ask every semester in my "Writing from Experience" course: How do you know that the writing you read comes from genuine experience and is not just b.s.? I tell them that for me the question is nearly irrelevant: If I am "moved" (emotionally and intellectually) by the writing, I respond favorably to it. From a writer's perspective, the act of reflecting experience on the page is in some sense an act of fiction. From the artful selection of details to the inevitable filtering of memory, writers who write about their lives compose their lives. In short, what I try to do is complicate the (naive) connection between a writer's "experience" and the words on the page.

So far, we have identified the following traits that make the narrative powerful: its manipulation of audience; its carefully crafted use of conversational rhythms; its truthfulness; and the presence of a distinctive voice on the page. Carol and Diane note as well that the narrator is a fine observer, suggesting the writer's ability to conjure up vivid and calculated scenes (all the evidence of the corpse's decay and neglect, for example). We can make the case that this narrative meets the standards set forth by our list of primary traits, as I try to do for the group:

> We do have a strong perspective here, and we do have a level of detail that is very striking. . . . how the words have an impact on the audience that's also expressed in the structure [or logic] of the piece. This isn't haphazardly put together. . . . It builds up as Pat says to a really touching conclusion. And the grammar and mechanics seem to be pretty sound.

In saying this, I can't help believing that the qualities that make this piece powerful transcend our primary traits: Kathy calls those qualities "directness" and "engagement." As a result, I also wonder whether I would convince that colleague in the chemistry(or psychology or history) department that this student's narrative shows promise for writing done in other disciplines. Perhaps Peter is right in that respect: reading, like writing, may be an act of faith.

8 What Is Good Writing?

> The truly knowledgeable person realizes that it is very hard to say something simply.
>
> —Diane

As we begin in earnest the process of reviewing the primary traits, Jerry reminds us that the original purpose of the list was to help us as tutors of writing, reflecting the order and priorities of our response to students' writing: we read for a sense of the writer's perspective initially and then for a sense of audience and the inclusion of appropriate evidence. But, as Peter notes, "we've gotten quite a bit beyond this" since—beyond both in the purpose of the document and in our thinking about its contents. The traits still guide us as tutors, providing us with a structure and vocabulary for response. But now they also serve a broader purpose and a more inclusive audience: they represent to students and to colleagues what we consider to be the qualities of competent writing.

In addition, much now seems left off the list, qualities that contribute mightily to the power of a piece of writing. Jerry, for one, wonders whether, in light of our discussions, we should include an awareness of multiple perspectives when defining good writing. I wonder whether this is another way of describing what the rhetorics used to call "acknowledging your opponent's point of view." In order to bolster your own argument, the textbooks told us, you need to recognize and counter the argument on the other side. But that was done only to raise your own flag, triumphant, at the end. Our discussion, on the other hand, has led us in another direction: we have been saying that thoughtful writing has a polyphonic quality, containing a tissue of perspectives as well as a range of voices. Good writing lays bare a variety of perspectives not to explode alternative points of view but rather to acknowledge the mingling of ideas or the heteroglossia against which we voice our own perspectives (Bakhtin 1981). Yet how can we articulate this quality in such a way as to make it a useful tool for evaluating and responding to a piece of writing? It's a daunting but fascinating task.

It occurs to me as well that in privileging a multiplicity of perspectives as a quality of good college writing, we facilitate our students' development as complex and synthetic thinkers. In the process, we would be tying students' writing to their cognitive development.

A practical manifestation of such development may be a writer's ability to use skillfully the words and ideas of another. Most if not all of us have felt frustrated by students' inability to write using texts other than their own. In our lab we have seen research papers that amount to nothing more than a string of quotations from barely read sources. Or we have seen students "borrow" wholesale a writer's words and ideas with no attempt to acknowledge a debt. For some of us, the difficulty may be tied to students' lack of familiarity with conventions of acknowledging and citing sources. For others of us—I include myself here—the difficulty goes deeper: students' naive notions as to how knowledge is made and expressed and their lack of experience in the kind of writing that calls for them to synthesize the ideas of others. How do we bring students to the point at which they can knowledgeably and skillfully weave expert testimony together with their own findings and perspective? How do we talk about the writing that emerges from that process? What, in other words, is that quality in writing that reveals the words and ideas of others while promoting the writer's own agenda?

Answers to those questions, if they come at all, are going to have to wait, because Peter has his own particular slant on what ought to be considered requisite for "good writing" and the group begins to engage him on that point:

> *Peter:* I think the ability to make the difficult simple, the ability to make the complex clear. . . .This is the hardest thing in the world to do . . . . Young writers think that difficult ideas must be expressed in a difficult way. They seem to think it's almost a necessity.
>
> *Diane:* Can that be a technique to stimulate discussion? Sometimes when I don't understand the words, it stimulates me to research, when I realize that I'm not on the same plane of understanding. There are people who use those large words and they are perfectly clear to them.
>
> *Howard:* It's true that when students come into our courses, they are so naive about the terminology that it becomes an extra challenge for the teacher . . .
>
> *Marlene:* But how much do you have to break it down?

Peter's insistence on the world "simplicity" (rather than clarity) throws us for a loop. Diane, Marlene, and I construe that word to mean language so reduced and simplified as to become something quite different from what it was. Quite possibly Peter might be speaking of an economy of expression. In a handout given to his writing and literature students on his own elements of style (and which he shares with us), Peter begins with "Say the most in the fewest words." "Write freely," he goes on, "and then cut." And yet there are moments in that same list when Peter seems to be aiming for writing that has the accessibility of speech. "Use words from your everyday speech," he advises, "words you are comfortable with." Peter seems to be aiming for prose that carries, as he puts it, the "sound of sense"—an accessible and engaging style.

Peter apparently sees little use for difficulty. In some ways, his students (those "young writers") may have a more realistic view of writing in college than Peter himself does. They know that the reading assigned by their teachers has meaning for their teachers; it speaks to them. And in order to succeed in those courses, students must master some of the conventions of those courses or, we might say, those discourse communities.

Diane raises the point that difficulty may have a purpose, a justification. Language may challenge us because ideas challenge us. "There are things," she reminds us, "that aren't that simple." "The truly knowledgeable person," she observes, "realizes that it is very hard to say something simply." As far as communicating knowledge to others is concerned, if our audience shares our assumptions and terms then we have little need to provide a glossary.

Marlene shares Diane's view that the language that we use in our classrooms has a genuine purpose. Her question, however—"But how much do you have to break it down?"—suggests the pressures that we all face to "break it down," that is, to simplify our materials (some, more cynically, might call it "dumbing down" our teaching). At the community college, where the expressed mission is to produce not merely historians or physicists but generally educated citizens, should not our language be less the specialists' and more the generalists'? Should open access refer not only to our admission policy but also to the words that we use in our classrooms and require students to read in our texts?

As I ask these questions, I am struck by how often discussions of this kind themselves become reduced to meaningless dichotomies. At the community college, the question often is raised: Are we training our students for the academy or for the workplace? Rarely do we consider the option of doing both. In "breaking down" the rich complexity of our subject areas, might we not be undermining our mission to educate generally a literate citizenry?

I engage Peter on his notion of "simplicity" by asking whether for our students the reading of poetry would be considered "simple." In doing so, I am offering the reading and critiquing of a poem as a specialized, discipline-specific mode of inquiry, with its own assumptions and apparatus. Diane chimes in by saying that many people ask, "Why can't [the poet] say it so that I can understand it?" Her point is not that poetry has little use at our college, but rather that poetry has its unique demands, which to those outside the poetry-reading community appear terribly complex. Peter responds by turning to Frost:

> When I say simplicity I mean simplicity beyond complexity. I don't mean simplemindedness. . . .Simplicity lures you into something, it coaxes you. . . . Take someone like Frost. . . . He gives you something simple that lures you in and he has something at the end that doesn't quite work as a cliché. You begin to pull it and the poem begins to unravel. And it becomes something profound.

Diane, when hearing this, admits "I'm not even sure what simple means anymore." "You talk about a simple poem," she adds, "and yet you have to reread and reread it: what is clarity then? what is simple?" Trying to make himself understood, Peter turns to Jerry, a mathematician, and asks whether a similar concept applies in his field. "Don't mathematicians refer to a theorem's 'elegance,' a stripping away of the extraneous to get to the heart of a theory or problem?" he asks. Jerry agrees but notes that there are several specialties of mathematics and if the theorem is "not in your field it may not be clear."

Trying to explore Peter's claim further, Pat, very interestingly, draws upon her own field, as well as Diane's, to shed light on the problem. Perhaps reading a poem, she says, is similar to the way people in her own field and in Diane's view the human body: the works are hidden but knowable. In other words, our experience and training allow us access that is denied to those without such a background.

Marlene, clearly attracted to the idea that students should write economically, wonders whether we could include economy of expression to our traits. Students are not saying what they mean simply and clearly. Peter, borrowing from Thoreau, refers to an "economy of spirit," a precise and economical expending of energy that invites "layers of richness and . . . gives body to simple prose."

Granted the complexity of Peter's call for simplicity and economy, nevertheless such a call runs counter to what people in composition have been saying for some time: that students so often are uncomfortable with written expression that they may need to be given confidence and fluency before we ask that they achieve conciseness of expression. In a certain sense, Peter's message is contradictory, seeming on the one hand to call for a kind of fluency or conversational quality in student writing while at the same time arguing for an almost poetic economy.

It is clear that whatever revisions we make to our document, we will emphasize the "sound of sense," as Peter puts it. That is, we will need to acknowledge the power of writing that has the immediacy of the human voice. Marlene is clearly taken by Peter's "write as if a human voice is speaking." Diane offers this caveat, however: "It depends on whom you're speaking to. You can speak to a group of historians and use one voice. If you're speaking to a group of students you might use another." In other words, "voice" may indeed be a construct shaped in part by the demands of the rhetorical situation, including the audience whom we are addressing.

Marlene complicates things further by noting that, even as we struggle to speak with the same language, abundant differences exist within departments and disciplines. In her own department there are "big differences," reflected most obviously in the textbooks assigned. "If I had to use the one book that everybody was using," she says, "I might quit." Although she does not say this, I suspect that she is referring to ongoing battles over revamping the old Western civilization course in favor of a more diverse or pluralistic perspective on history.

In hearing Marlene speak about the lack of standardized or stable knowledge within disciplines, Peter observes that much of that difference may be due to the differences of background and training among community college faculty. He notes that in the English department there may be colleagues with master's degrees in professional writing and others with Ph.D.'s in English literature. Put those people together and you may see disagreement about the way we teach the use of evidence or logic in our writing courses, he says.

Of course, these differences might very well account for much of the disagreement that Marlene sees within departments at the two-year college. And given the inevitable aging of community college faculty and recent initiatives to hire more and more young faculty (among them Ph.D.'s), even greater rifts may develop among faculty on matters of pedagogical and disciplinary expertise.

A case in point might very well be in the habit of some faculty in English and beyond to insist on writing as bound to a clear and unequivocal thesis. That term, which has suffered through much abuse since the days of the process movement (so aligned was it with the five-paragraph theme), was left out of our earlier document simply because it might be misunderstood and be taken as producing formulaic writing. "Can't we say," asks Marlene, "that good writing must have a strongly worded thesis—even in a narrative?" Peter, relying on a rhetorical tradition, replies that a narrative might not, strictly speaking, have a thesis. We may have to make a distinction among argumentative, expository, and narrative writing in order to retain "perspective" (and its component term "thesis") as a broad, generalizable quality of "good writing."

And yet, having said that, Peter agrees that the writing that we require students to do ought to reveal the writer's way of seeing the world. That said, we all agree that "perspective" ought to be highlighted in our document. But what is the relationship between "perspective" and "point of view," and "voice," for that matter? Peter offers, in writing, his take on all of this:

> I believe "perspective" means a way of looking. . . . Perspectives cannot be stated, strongly or otherwise. . . . "Voice" is the personality of the writer on the page. "Point of view" is the attitude, the inclination, with which the subject is approached. "Thesis" is the arguable opinion.

To render the discussion more concrete, Peter takes the subject of abortion:

> A perspective would be the moral landscape of abortion. My voice is the person writing this. The point of view is the place where you stand and look, where you're coming from, your preconceptions—whether I'm a born-again Christian, a Catholic. . . . What I'm going to say about it, that's my thesis.

Leaving aside the problems implicit in linking "voice" with "the person writing," we do feel that Peter's analysis makes a great deal of sense, especially in its separation of conceptual framework (point of view) and the position to be argued (thesis).

Our discussion of perspective leads naturally to consider the matter of evidence, since, we can infer from Peter's gloss, "where you're coming from" shapes what you see. Now, in our earlier document, we had assumed a unanimity of opinion about the nature of evidence, not taking any pains to problematize it: ". . . good writing must marshal evidence or support." What is evidence, anyway? Is what passes for evidence in one field the same as what is accepted in another? If so, what would account for evidence in the narrative about Lou's death? So often we assume (as do the textbooks) that evidence is used to buttress an argument, a means of persuasion. Can a narrative—or this particular narrative—be considered persuasive? Diane, for one, feels that it can. Speaking of our student writer, she says: "He was trying to persuade us that he had an experience that was profoundly affecting and he persuaded [us] that that was so."

Peter, in response, asks, "Why not say the purpose of narrative writing is to move? Of argumentative writing to persuade?" In these terms, narrative detail may support the writer's intention to move readers in a powerful way.

Kathy, concerned that we are forgetting the obvious function of writing to express and produce "good thinking," is afraid that we are reducing the complex purpose of writing to a few categories. In addition to moving or persuading, writing, she says, allows us to monitor our own learning. It is an excellent point because it forces us to include the effect of writing on the writer as well as on the reader. Peter, helping to craft our consensus, suggests this statement: "Good writing makes use of detail to persuade, to move, or to inform." How far we have come from the tentative and partial version of our earlier document ("If the intent is to persuade the reader, good writing must marshal evidence or support").

As far as the other traits are concerned, a broad consensus already exists on the matters of "logic" and "correctness." However, at Carol's request, we remove the rather condescending description of "correctness" in our earlier version (with its qualifier "generally" and the reductive quotation marks around "correct") and produce a much cleaner statement: "Good writing displays competency in grammar and punctuation and accuracy in spelling." Added to this, by insistence of the group, is a caveat about acknowledging sources: "The use of another's words or ideas must always be cited."

That last addition reflects the concern of many that students are not using sources responsibly or thoughtfully. My own feeling is that the issue goes much deeper than citation of sources—to the complex process of synthesizing source materials. Marlene, for one, identifies this as a problem that cuts across all disciplines: "I see students who can't synthesize the material. It's like a beaded necklace that they string along. A paragraph on this one, a paragraph on that one. And they can't put it together." Kathy insists that the ability to synthesize ought best to be handled in our particular fields and departments. As far as our students are concerned, they need to recognize the need to cite sources, which is indeed a matter of "correctness" or technique. Her view carries the room. I can't say that I'm especially happy that we have "ghettoized" the problem of using sources, but perhaps this is just a start of a discussion about the process.

Although we agree to relegate the discussion of synthesizing sources to departments and programs, we nevertheless continue to maintain the usefulness of establishing generalized or primary traits necessary for competent college writing. We decide to keep the five broad categories from our earlier list: perspective, audience, evidence, logic, and correctness. However, we see fit to alter dramatically the descriptors for each term. Here then are the revised traits:

Primary Traits

The writing lab staff has come to a consensus about good writing which establishes usable criteria to evaluate the writing that we will read in the lab.

A consensus as to what makes good writing should begin with this qualifier, however: *writing is contextual.* By that we mean that writing depends on the disciplinary context and the situation in which it is done. Each discipline does have a distinct set of assumptions about the way knowledge is made and expressed. A student who writes an essay for an English literature course may be ruled by conventions and assumptions quite unlike those that guide the student writing for a history course.

Nevertheless, we have come to a consensus on those qualities in writing that cut across areas of expertise and knowledge. These are considered "primary traits," usable criteria to evaluate the many kinds of writing that may come our way.

Perspective: Good writing has perspective, a way of seeing. Perspective is expressed through point of view, voice, and thesis:

> *point of view* reveals the experience, the knowledge and the inclination of the writer;
>
> *voice* expresses the writer's personality on the page;
>
> *thesis* establishes the writer's main idea.

Audience: Good writing is appropriate to the reader, the purpose, and the occasion.

Evidence: Good writing makes use of detail to persuade, to move, or to inform the reader.

Logic: Good writing is coherent from sentence to sentence, paragraph to paragraph, beginning to end.

Correctness: Good writing displays competency in grammar and punctuation, and accuracy in spelling. The use of another's words or ideas must always be cited.

No doubt such a list runs the risk of abuse, that is, of being employed as a bare-bones checklist and reducing the complexity of any writing task. But we feel it important at least to try to articulate, in language that crosses disciplines, a consensus on what constitutes competent writing at our college. Significantly, our new list argues that all writing expresses a perspective, whether that writing be an argumentative essay in English or an observer's notebook in astronomy. Moreover, the evidence that marks competent college writing may move as well as persuade an audience. In other words, powerful narratives may lay claim to offering evidence as much as do analytical, argumentative, and expository writing. Distinctions between transactional and expressive kinds of writing therefore become blurred. Expressive writing is not without its own purposes, agendas, and supportive materials. It has, in other words, a legitimacy equal to other kinds of writing currently privileged in the classroom.

9 Seeing Ourselves as Experts

> I explained to [an ESL] student that there are different ways of thinking. He said, "I like the way you think in this country and I would like to think that way myself."
>
> —Diane

For this group, comprising teacher/tutors whose students display a wide array of writing problems, discussions of student writing must yield specific strategies and protocols to help those students. When all is said and done, we want to find a way to identify what problems reside in their writing and then direct them to find possible solutions. In other words, there has always been in these sessions a very practical, indeed urgent agenda: let's produce strategies for both our teaching and our tutoring that will work.

Perhaps such a goal has been impractical in itself, given the disparate expectations that all of us have within our own classrooms, our own disciplines. But the wondrous thing about our writing center, and this workshop, is that we have an opportunity and an inclination to find a common language. That has been clear from the start. The discussion surrounding our "primary traits" indicates as much. Can we now, also, find some common ground when describing what ought to happen when we tutor students who come to our writing lab? Can we agree on both our objectives and our methods as tutors?

Any discussion of our tutor protocol must begin with the problematic nature of our roles as teacher/tutors. Each of us is a classroom teacher as well as a writing lab tutor. Are our roles as teachers and tutors mutually exclusive, with nothing being transferred from one to the other? Indeed, since as teachers we are accustomed to wielding power over our students' texts through our grading, is it possible that our experience in the classroom may hinder our performance as tutors? May we not be tempted to compel students to write our own versions of papers rather than the students'? I prefer to think, following Helon Raines's view, that our teaching may benefit from our assuming the role of tutor, while our tutoring—certainly in a lab that invites writing from all of the disciplines—benefits from our experience and expertise as teachers (1994). By that I mean that, on the one hand, as teachers we benefit from playing a tutor's facilitative role—allowing students to retain ownership over their own writing, as we writing teachers say. On the other hand, as teachers we bring a disciplinary knowledge and the credibility that comes from such expertise.

Anyone who has been involved in a writing center knows the importance of credibility to its standing among faculty, students, and administrators (North 1984).

What ought to be our objectives going into a tutoring session and what kinds of behavior will most effectively allow us to satisfy those objectives? Unfortunately, early attempts to render a tutoring protocol (by another faculty team) yielded only a description of procedure: Read the students' file, ask for the assignment, determine deadlines, and so forth. What this group needs to do is examine aspects of writing pedagogy and produce a document that will help guide all of us to become effective tutors. That said, any account of how tutoring ought to occur must value the "situatedness" of each tutoring session. Just as evaluation of writing cannot be ripped out of the disciplinary context that generates it, so tutoring sessions reflect a unique set of circumstances and expectations and cannot be standardized or reduced.

Diane, who, by virtue of a leave of absence, has had the luxury of serving on two faculty teams, informs the group that the initial purpose for establishing a tutoring protocol (and a list of primary traits) was to ease the anxiety felt by faculty in departments other than English about tutoring writing in the first place. Those pioneering faculty were questioning themselves, Diane says: "Who am I? Why am I doing this? What we did was share the kinds of things that went on, so all of us felt we were on the same wavelength. We didn't feel that we had that kind of expertise." Such a protocol needed to emerge from the faculty's own stories, told, reflected upon and discussed back and forth—rather than a directive given from top (read English department) down (read all other departments). As with the traits, this had to be a joint effort in order to be credible.

In our reading from the night before, Emily Meyer and Louise Z. Smith (1987) had prompted us to think about the qualities distinguishing experienced writers from novices that we would like to promote in the students whom we tutor. Practiced writers, they tell us, develop an "inner monitor, another 'self'" that

> comments and questions as the writing self sets down ideas, and it is
> this voice that helps the writer specify and connect . . . ideas. [Inex-
> perienced writers] leave out crucial information, producing prose that
> is elliptical or "writer-based," as opposed to prose that is directed to a
> reader, or "reader-based" [Flower]. (27, 28)

Drawing from Linda Flower's study of writing as a cognitive process, Meyer and Smith see experienced writers as capable of achieving critical distance from their writing—adopting the stance of the reader—while novices remain within themselves, paying little heed to what impact their words might have on another.

When I mention to the group that in our tutoring sessions we might very well serve as restraining readers and thereby promote in writers a more critical "inner voice," Peter demonstrates little patience with the idea. "Sometimes," he says, "that inner voice is so damned developed you can't write a thing." Meyer and Smith, recognizing the problem, refer to "self-censoring writers," those writers who are unable to achieve fluency because they are too self-conscious about how their writing might "play" (44). But Peter's objections go deeper, I know. They have to do with a view of writers as true to their own visions and free to work out those visions without meddling from troublesome readers. In this respect, writing ought to be, in Peter Elbow and Jennifer Clarke's phrase, "desert island discourse" (1987, 19). Sometimes, perhaps early in the drafting process, writers ought to go at it alone, freely and creatively. Only later ought they to get reader feedback. Given (our) Peter's view, so often expressed at this workshop, that writers must first of all "tell the truth," I would think that he might downplay the importance of a reader entirely and privilege the writers' "truth." And yet Peter is, at *this* session, a tutor in our writing lab and a teacher who works terribly hard to encourage students to write productively.

In fact, we learn that in Peter's writing classes students read their writing aloud to the whole class for peer comments. In these sessions, students read their papers completely through before eliciting comments. When commentary begins, Peter demonstrates a response, especially early on in the course, by framing questions—questions that bring out what works and doesn't work about a piece of writing. Eventually, the students themselves will produce useful questions and comments. Writers pay heed to what their peers say because, as Peter puts it, "They care more about what their friends think than what the teacher will give them."

Even for Peter, then, writing can indeed be seen as a social process, a "conversation" between writers and readers. That process might be particularly appropriate for our students at the community college, too many of whom are isolated from one another, from their teachers, and from the institution. In part the reason for this may lie in the kinds of lives our students lead, shuttling between work and school. They simply don't have the time to stick around. Another reason may rest with the diversity of our students—differences of age, but also of culture, language, and ethnicity. Diane tells a story that reminds us how complicated our students are. A student came to the lab for advice on a piece of writing for an ESL class. Seeing potential in the writing, Diane suggested that he share his work with other students, family, and friends. The student then implied that he didn't feel comfortable doing so. For him, in fact, it was important not to share his writing with other ESL students especially. "I like the way you think in this country," he told Diane, "and I would like to think that way myself." Sharing his writing was difficult enough, but sharing his work with others of like experience seemed beside the point. He wanted to be assimilated quickly into the ways of the academy.

If there is a single lesson from Diane's story, it might be that effective tutoring sessions have to acknowledge the complex web of intentions behind a piece of writing. We need, in our protocol, to allow opportunity for writers to provide that context. Obviously we ought not to compel writers to accept our purposes as theirs. Our comments need to open up rather than close out conversation.

It occurs to me, as I reflect further on Diane's story, that it offers other lessons as well, going beyond tutoring concerns to raise broader issues of power and identity. The student who came to the lab for help with his writing was obviously coming for much more: he desired the means by which he could not only achieve assimilation within the dominant culture of school but also the power that he saw inevitably accompanying that assimilation. For all our politically correct desire to respect the differences that our students bring to our classes and our writing lab, we need to recognize indeed where power lies in those classes and in that writing lab: with teachers and tutors. Consequently, the aim to "become like" those teachers and tutors can be seen as both pragmatic and shrewd.

While our role is in part to help transform the composing process into a conversation (in effect to get writers to learn to talk to themselves as well as to readers about the writing), we are also demonstrating a critical stance ourselves in order to facilitate the very kind of assimilation that Diane's student devoutly wished. In other words, just as Peter feels comfortable demonstrating a critical response during peer student review, so we as tutors must acknowledge and use our own authority as expert readers (and teachers) within a given tutoring session. Essentially, that was what the ESL student was saying to Diane: You are an expert and I want to learn how you do it.

The student assumes, of course, that all of us who work in the lab have a justifiable claim as experts (as native English speakers but also as tutors of writing and experts in our particular specialties) and that all of us are comfortable in that role. He would be surprised, I think, by how ill at ease those of who work at two-year colleges are made to feel by that "expert" role. As has often been noted in this workshop, we prefer to see ourselves as generalists, suited by temperament and commitment to casting our nets wide rather than digging deep within a discipline. I have often been reminded of that uneasiness when the subject of our disciplinary expertise has come up in these sessions. Kathy's comments in particular seem to strike a note of defensiveness for me: "Maybe because I don't have a department. . . . I don't think as departmentally as you guys do." Thinking "departmentally" is in fact rarely done at our college, where department meetings offer little opportunity to discuss the content of what it is those departments actually do. Moreover, our relatively low status (and low pay) as teaching faculty (in sharp contrast with the profile and pay of our privileged colleagues at research institutions) has marked us off as nonspecialists and nonexperts. Our specialty, if that is what it can be called, is in the delivery of knowledge, not in knowledge itself.

I believe that what we do at the two-year college allows us to lay real claim to an expertise that goes beyond thinking "departmentally" and that transcends equally our roles as experts in instruction only. What might that expertise be?

I suspect that our expertise as two-year college faculty may best be brought out in settings such as writing centers and writing-in-the-disciplines projects (as opposed to writing-across-the curriculum projects, which have tended to gloss over important differences in the way disciplines write and think). In such settings, we two-year college faculty may engage in transdisciplinary conversations without feeling as if we have betrayed departmental or disciplinary affiliations. Two-year college writing centers staffed by full-time faculty from a variety of academic areas may be valuable sites for disciplinary research. As I have often written, we are predisposed to cross borders.

That said, we too rarely have an opportunity to reflect on the nature of expert knowledge and ways of knowing that we bring to such conversations. In that sense, we are like our students, not sufficiently practiced in "thinking about thinking."

———————

We can make the argument that when students become tutors of their peers' writing, they, too, must acknowledge the expertise that they bring to the "exchange," and visualize their own behavior as demonstrating a critical response for inexperienced writers. This view of peer response in some ways answers Marlene's concern. She worries that students simply don't know how to critique writing—their own or others'—effectively. It is, of course, one thing to hear this view from a faculty tutor; it's quite another to hear it echoed by one of our peer tutors. Deb, a student who tutors in our lab, does exactly that when she says: "You need someone you could really trust. Who will dig deep enough but not rip totally apart. I don't think you can find this in a classroom [that is, in fellow students]. You get no critique whatsoever." The fact is that when students acquire the experience and training to assist less experienced student writers, they have distinguished themselves from their peers. Moreover, Kenneth Bruffee, who has eloquently defended the notion that knowledge is made, and shared, among peers, has himself recognized that there are those who are inside knowledge communities and those who are outside, and that those on the outside rely on the "linguistic improvisation" of specially gifted translators. Although Bruffee does not refer specifically to peer tutors (but only to the traditional "teachers" and "students") we can reasonably infer that what he says applies to trained student tutors as well as to teachers:

> Teachers have to be able to translate at the community boundaries that they belong to and uncountable numbers of nonacademic, non-professional communities that their students belong to. . . .
> Mastering the linguistic improvisation involved in this third kind of nonstandard discourse—negotiation between knowledge communities and outsiders who want to join them—distinguishes a knowledge community's teachers from its ordinary members. (1993, 64, 65)

Although tutors in a given writing lab may not be faculty, they are invested with a certain authority and bring a certain expertise to tutoring sessions with students. Moreover, peer tutors too may find themselves in the role of translators—of teachers' comments and instructions—for students not yet initiated in the ways of a particular discipline or of the academy generally.

Bruffee's use of the phrase "third kind of nonstandard discourse" is reminiscent of what Meyer and Smith mention in our reading: that tutors need to find an effective language by which to inform students of academic and disciplinary conventions, and which holds currency for those students. Meyer and Smith reduce the language issue to the difference between asking "How can you illustrate your topic sentence?" and "Why do you think this?" (1987, 30). Aside from the need to ask open-ended questions (preventing a co-opting of students' writing), they recommend that tutors use "everyday language" in discussing writing with students. The issue is not that simple, of course. Even "everyday language" may take on considerable complexity, depending on the context. Consider an exchange that the members of our group have about what constitutes "persuasive" evidence:

Howard: Isn't all good writing persuasive?

Kathy: That's a loaded term, though.

Diane: Even that experience of Peter's student is persuasive [referring to the student narrative discussed earlier]. He was trying to persuade us that he had had an experience that was profoundly affecting and he persuaded the reader that that was so.

Kathy: But a lot of rhetoric books use that term to mean argument.

Peter: Why not say the purpose of narrative writing is to move? Of argumentative writing to persuade?

Kathy: Could we say something about anecdote as support?

Peter's attempt to negotiate our different readings of the word "persuade" seems to be successful (and will wind up in our new version of the traits). Nevertheless, Kathy is attempting here to complicate our sense of both "persuade" and "evidence." Might these terms not include the validation that derives from personal observation and experience?

The issue of what kind of language to use in tutoring sessions, then, is an important and complex one. As tutors we need to use language that bridges the gulf between the discourse communities which students aim to enter and the community or communities to which they already belong. Perhaps our own struggles to cross the disciplinary borders that separate us have been good preparation for aiding our students' journeys of translation.

Our discussion of a tutoring protocol, then, yields the following principles that we believe should underlie the tutoring done at the lab, together with tutoring behaviors that emerge from those principles:

Tutor Protocol

All writing is prompted by, and takes meaning from, a specific situation or task.

> Always ask students to produce their teachers' instructions and/or guidelines.
>
> Discuss teachers' comments, if any, about the writing.
>
> Serve as mediator between teachers' stated or unstated expectations and students' understanding of those expectations.

The overall goal of tutoring writing is to promote in our students a reader's perspective on their work.

> Have students read their writing aloud.
>
> Fashion questions and comments that are reader-based, offering writers a critical perspective on their work.

Students need to play prominent and active roles in the revision of their writing (to maintain their roles as authors of that writing).

> Ask students to explain in their own words what the prompt is asking and what they want to get out of the tutoring session.
>
> Ask open-ended questions that facilitate rather than co-opt student revision.

Tutors need to adopt a contextualized and yet accessible language in responding to students' writing.

> Use clear and jargon-free language when discussing students' writing.
>
> When responding, take your cue from the writing prompt.
>
> Always situate commentary in the writing itself, rather than "rubber-stamping" the same responses from paper to paper.

No tutor protocol ought to be prescriptive, demanding that tutors follow these strategies slavishly. Indeed, just as writing acquires meaning from the writing scene or situation, so tutoring writing must be similarly contextualized and situated. No two tutoring sessions are alike. However, as a group, we feel strongly that the broad principles that underlie the practice have a special currency regardless of the tutoring moment.

Closing: Telling Our Story

> In general, we have all come to accept the fact that what we do is generally misunderstood by the academy.
>
> —Janice Albert

> There is no general story to be told, no synoptic picture to be had.
> . . . What we can construct, if we keep notes and survive, are hindsight accounts of the connectedness of things that seem to have happened: pieced-together patternings, after the fact.
>
> —Clifford Geertz

It would seem to be an easy task: to explain to the academy at large what we two-year college faculty do. After all, we are products of academic (read four-year) institutions. But so often when speaking to colleagues at four-year schools we are put into Janice Albert's situation: "I have tried to get them to say 'community college,' but it always comes out 'junior'" (1994, 10). We are simply not taken seriously as academics—that is, as scholars or researchers. In their eyes, our work has little to do with the life of the mind. In large part, this book represents an effort to represent community college faculty as deeply reflective and impassioned practitioners.

But, like all journeys that cross borders, this effort, I realize, brings with it great challenges. Have I adequately represented the two-year college teacher and institution? Or have I somehow distorted what I heard and saw to fit my own peculiar bias? Indeed, can I rightly say that I represent those two-year colleagues "back home" at all? Do I want to? Despite nine years of full-time teaching at my two-year college, I remain uncertain about playing such a role. Reviewers' comments on this manuscript, while most helpful, seem to highlight my ambivalence. One reviewer reminds me of the need to locate this work "within a framework that speaks to community college teaching/pedagogy issues" in light of the "significant responsibility" that I have to represent two-year college faculty's "professional and personal concerns." Another reviewer would like me to bring out more clearly certain "issues of teaching in community colleges." These are reasonable demands, to be sure, especially in light of the scarcity of published works authentically representing two-year college faculty.

But, at the same time, I feel the need to speak on behalf of and to all faculty, at two- or four-year schools, who struggle with the issues that we were struggling with during those three weeks in July: achieving perspective on our ways of knowing, reading, and writing; reflecting on the transformative powers of language, both written and spoken; offering our students ways of discovering the truth of things amid the conditional and contingent; and translating our expertise into social action. These are causes that unite all teachers, regardless of level or institution. In portraying two-year college faculty as participants in such a conversation, I hope to bring two-year colleges within the academic fold, rather than to isolate two-year colleges from other segments of higher education. I fear that any further isolation of that sort can only serve to foster more misunderstanding on all sides.

And yet much of what we had to say in those three weeks did seem to address the unique concerns of two-year college faculty: reconciling our specialized knowledge with the two-year college's commitment to general and comprehensive education; initiating students who have had little success in school into the academic enterprise; and reconceiving our work to include both scholarship and teaching.

The fact of the matter is that too few community college teachers are writing about the work that they do. Too often we and our work are constructed by others rather than by ourselves. It is indeed time for more of us who teach at the two-year college level to write about our work: to present papers and to publish. And to do so with confidence and poise.

If my own writing can serve as evidence, however, the task of "getting it right" will be formidable. As I reflect on what I have written about that summer (now more than two years ago), I suspect that I have made it into something quite different from what it was. I felt compelled to piece it all together as seamlessly as possible. Moreover, I felt the need to "situate" this conversation within the ongoing conversations of teachers outside the room, to demonstrate that our concerns may have application beyond the walls of our own particular classrooms and institution. Do not misunderstand what I am saying (and yet how easy it is to be "misunderstood"): the voices that made their way into the document were those that I heard during those three weeks, duly recorded and, oh so laboriously, transcribed. But, as they say, you had to be there: these sessions were more passionate—and digressive—than the story I have told.

Why did I tell the story in the first place? Why not simply be content with what we said and did during those three weeks? As I have said, it is time for two-year college teachers to construct themselves rather than merely to let others do the constructing. It is time to demonstrate both to ourselves and to others that our work and our reflection on that work have an impressive depth and scope.

To a person, each of us remained a determined generalist, committed to the idea of promoting a generally educated citizenry, each of us clinging to the hope that the picket fences of our particular disciplines might be removed and a common ground revealed.

And yet accompanying that view has been an acknowledgment that perhaps good fences do make good neighbors. Each of us looks at the world through a distinct set of lenses, and has much to offer the other, if only we can articulate what we see and how we see it. This is the rub, of course. So internalized have our disciplines' modes of thinking become that we all struggled during these three weeks to become more cognizant of perceptual frames, the paradigms that govern how we see and think.

We struggled as well when asked to step outside the comfortable zones of our own expertise. Perhaps we needed to feel that discomfort, to slip into the shoes of the uninitiated. We gained from doing so in part because the experience sensitized us to the plight of our students, who labor mightily to decipher the strange languages of the academy.

After the fact, the story of these three weeks can be seen as merely an account of what happened among the people in that room at that time (indeed, one unhappy reviewer of this manuscript likened the work to a "diary of a small circle of friends"). But, having said that, I am reminded of the point made early in the workshop: "All macrohistory is autobiography." As I mentioned earlier, I tried to tell our story within the context of stories told by teachers outside our college, all of which could make up an even larger narrative about what it means to be reflective practitioners.

"It is difficult to know what to do with the past," writes Clifford Geertz, attempting to undermine our clichéd assumptions both that we can capture the past and that we ought to use it productively (1995, 165). And yet, as even Geertz admits, we are enthralled by the opportunity to trace the footprints that memory has left behind. Perhaps the stories that we tell have uses despite their incompleteness. Perhaps they can offer both hope and a sense of renewal. Above all, that may be the legacy of those three weeks in July.

Appendix: What Each Discipline Wants—A Conversation

Transcript of a conversation with Peter (here designated as "P"), Pat (PM), Howard (H), Kathy (K), Diane (D), Marlene (M), Carol (CM), Jerry (J), Chris (CG), and Greg (G), our lab assistant.

P: A girl came up and told me, "My brother said I shouldn't waste time with this class: Why should I take this class?"

H: What was the course?

P: American lit.

H: What was the answer?

P: At the time it was after the riots in L.A.; a kid was talking about a drive-by shooting. I don't know if he participated in one, and the interviewer said what if it had been your children? and the kid said, So what? It's better to die than to live. That was touching something really wrong with their lives, with people. What's the answer? There's got to be some answer. "It's better to live than die." I said that's what I'm going to discover. Some of the best minds in American literature can give us an affirmation that will make us believe that it is better to live than to die. And that's what I'm going to try to teach in this course. Can we give that kid some answer?

H: I hope that we've all of us asked ourselves what it is that excites us about what we teach and why we teach. That's a beautiful answer. Did she believe it?

P: At the end she wrote me a little letter. She did. Modesty forbids me to bring it.

H: Peter, I think the question that the student put to you is, I'm sure, a question many of our students are asking themselves when they come into our classes. It's a question that we ought to get in the habit of asking ourselves: What do we want our students to get out of our courses? In our journals for next time, let's try to ask the question: What do we want our students to come away with?

K: Why take this course?

H: Yes, and this will be a good exercise not only in journal keeping but in monitoring ourselves and our own learning.

P: I find myself [that] when doing an introduction to literature I tend to pursue those things that I myself need in my life. If those needs in me are that I am human and they are too. . . . I feel if I can speak to my own needs first that somehow a sense of urgency, passion comes through and that they respond.

H: Your own needs in the course that you are teaching?

D: I'd like to amend the question, not only why they take the course but why they take the course from *you*. What is it that you give to the course? What is it that you give to the course that would make the course more rewarding?

K: I don't feel a discipline as strongly as let's say a biologist or a chemist. At the two-year level, how many of our students are actually being asked to write as a historian writes? or asked to write as a psychologist writes? And even the nursing plan has the special characteristics but it's quite human, it's quite readable, easy to deal with . . . . And some of this higher-level engineering [as described in an essay by Lee Odell, 1992] seems to be at another level of education.

H: What's your question? Can you phrase your question?

K: How much of this is going to be practical at the two-year college? How much of this will we need to deal with at the two-year college?

H: It's a good question.

M: I think the relevance is important because . . . the people don't know, how am I to communicate. . . .

K: But I think that's an easier level. Even in some of the English and nursing.

D: The thing that I underlined was, what it goes back to again is the written assignment. If the student comes to you with a written assignment that is explicit, as soon as you had a few key words here you'd know what the problem was. . . . I think the key to knowing what each discipline wants is knowing what the [purpose of the] assignment is. Is it to criticize? Is it to write a poem on your own? Is it to critique a certain character in the book? If the student isn't doing what the assignment is asking for, you're off-base.

K: I can deal with that, and I understand that. But it's a question of audience too. When you're taking a psychology class here, you are not going to write an article for a psychology journal to be read by other psychologists.

H: Isn't that what Chris's assignments are?

K: That's what I'm asking. What is the level that we're expecting? You see the level many of our students come in at. Even in the lab, from what I've seen, they are really so far from being able to analyze a historical event as a historian or analyze an experience as a psychologist.

M: My experience in the lab is that people shut down. . . . I can't do this. I can't even think. Do it for me.

K: I don't think that's my question. Do you understand my question?

H: Yes, let me think if I can rephrase it. This is something that each of us wrestles with. When we teach our students are we aiming for some kind of general skill? Or are we training them to read literature, to write a particular kind of memo, or to be historians? to get a kind of historical perspective? Or training them to think like mathematicians? or dental hygienists or nurses? Where do we aim? Are we trying to give them some kind of specific knowledge?

P: Each discipline, it seems to me, has particular metaphors that apply, ways of speaking of people and actions, the world, explorations of ethics. Where psychologists see the world and society in one way, the English teacher looks at it another way. They're all using different metaphors, a structure of reality in a particular discipline. And I think if you can pick up the metaphor as a historian you can aid the student not so much to write as a historian but to write in a way which will facilitate that student's expression as well as making it congenial to his reader. . . .

H: Behind the metaphor are there actual different conceptual demands? different ways of thinking?

P: I think they go with the metaphors. . . . they change, they are evolving. At certain times there are generally accepted ways of proceeding in a discipline.

K: But I'm reminded of what Diane said yesterday. People forget how much you've learned since you got your master's. Can you expect that student in the first literature course to have bought into all that training and tradition about which you now speak with such ease?

P: Without giving them a reason and way it is possible to inspire [them] to move into a particular line . . . and what happens is that you begin to do it in that fashion . . . students will be working with that metaphor, in that mode. I don't think you can always do it but you can make them comfortable with the subject.

H: The fact is we've been trained in a certain way to think and to look at the world from our own very distinct perspectives. We may not articulate what is necessary to be a nurse, or historian. The things we have students read, the things we say in class may suggest it. I guess that's one of the assumptions behind this article. The question you're raising is [whether] at a two-year college we ought to be giving students something different, more general.

CM: It goes back to lowering our standards. . . . I think if we expect more of them they will try to produce more.

K: I don't think I'm saying that we have to expect less. What [Peter is] saying is frightening because I then as a tutor have to know the metaphors of all those disciplines. . . . Really I thought the paper had to make sense to me. I'm a literate person. That's the level I was working at. If it were a discrete [assignment] and there were certain guidelines I think that should be in the assignment. It still should make sense to me. . . . I'm not an engineer and I'm not reading it as an engineer. . . .

H: If the teacher makes it clear what kinds of thinking are being required in the assignment itself then our jobs become easier. The student gains some access to what the teacher is asking for. . . .

M: Can you come up with a concrete example because I think this is so abstract I'm having trouble with it.

We discuss an assignment from an engineering course, as given in Lee Odell's "Context-Specific Ways of Knowing and the Evaluation of Writing" (1992).

D: On page 92, left-hand side . . . I think what you're saying Kathy is, would we be seeing this kind of high technology. . . .

K: This could be clearly explained in the assignment or what the student was told to do. . . .

H: Interestingly, there were two different responses to the same assignment. The teacher did not make explicit what he was asking for. . . .

D: The assignment was a design description . . .

K: But I think the key here in this distinction [is] what were the expectations of the writing?

D: If the assignment is clear no matter what the language I feel very comfortable helping the student. I don't care what area it's in.

K: I think this is really key to audience in my mind. Now I'm challenging you, Peter. . . .Even though I may not have the metaphor of a discipline I can still bring to the passage my perspective. I think that's valid. I shouldn't have to buy into your metaphors to see some strength in my interpretation.

P: That's true. But I meant metaphors in the broadest sense of the word. Part of it is clarity. If the metaphor is expressed in the assignment. Ah ha, this is the key word.

D: Peter's correct, I think. We went to a conference at Brown. . . . The whole focus was that the language of the profession is the picket fence that keeps out the uninitiated. Part of the course taking is as you go along they give you more of the language so that you understand what they are saying. So these two words were deliberately thrown in there—to make sure you will do more research . . .

K: At our level should we be keeping people out of this thinking, this understanding?

D: But, no, what we're beginning to do is to lead them through . . . so that they can go over the picket fences. . . . I don't think that's our role.

P: . . . because we have different ways of knowing . . . it's not just an explanation. It's something deep.

H: It's important for us to be able to talk to one another about what it is we look for in the work that are those ways of knowing from some other discipline. It's a real struggle.

P: . . . why does [a psychologist] see the way she does? We begin to understand her way of knowing. . . . It's what makes somebody clear.

H: How often do we think about how we think? How often do we think about what it is we are asking of our students in our areas? Do we do it in our assignments?

P: We do it instinctively . . .

D: I think some of the metaphors mask ignorance—of the person who's using them.

P: I'm not being understood. By metaphor I mean a way of structuring reality in order to get at a particular meaning, which both satisfies and excites. I don't mean metaphor in terms of stuffiness and rules . . .

D: . . . sometimes we use the terminology, the metaphors, because we don't have a better way of saying things. . . .

P: But I believe there are ways of saying things that can't be said in any other way. For instance, when Einstein talks about the space-time continuum that's a metaphor, not a scientific fact. . . , a way of understanding the world that is both satisfying and exciting and inspiring . . . until someone comes a long to say that the metaphor no longer operates. . . .

H: Unless we explain to ourselves what it is we are giving to our students and then explain in some kind of common language to others, to other teachers, what it is, then we are going to be sealed off and no one will be the better for it. . . .

G: The space-time continuum metaphor was designed to bridge the gap . . . to make what Einstein said accessible and not just to mathematicians. . . . Knowing the language of it doesn't mean you understand what you are saying.

H: I remember when we talked about what made for good writing in our disciplines [during the semester, Kathy] brought out certain models of thinking specific to different cultures. Some cultures are linear some are circular.

K: Peter just demonstrated what I'm saying. When he talked about [disciplinary knowledge as a] journey he used literature references but he did it in a manner that I understand him. I don't have to buy into all that experience and knowledge that he has. . . .

H: I think what's coming out is a kind of schizophrenia in our mission. Are we supposed to train our students as critics of literature or something more generalized? It's a battle I fight all the time in my intro. to lit. class. Some years ago I would have taught that class using purely literary terms . . . I don't do that anymore. I try to give them something else, something that may be transferred. I know there are people who teach English 12 very differently, very generalized or very literary. . . .

P: By being true to your discipline you make the work most relevant to your students. . . .I think the world is best perceived through one window. I think if you look through that one window as best as you can, you give your students . . . the truth that you have. What I offer is what I know best.

K: You said that you have to give them what you know, the truth as you see it, but you also have to give them what's relevant. So his not focusing on the literary terms is not changing the mission.

P: Don't look for relevance. Look for what you perceive to be truth and it will be relevant.

D: I was impressed with what [one of our peer tutors] said yesterday. He said he saw college as telling him how to live rather than how to make a living. What I'm going back to again is the assignment. If teachers know why the course they're teaching is important, if they make the assignments such that the student is introduced to the concepts or the truth then I don't think it's as difficult for us. . . . A lot of assignments that students do are meaningless exercises. So when we get them it becomes an exercise in futility because we don't know what the truth is.

H: The beauty of this is that we need to find a way to talk to one another. When a student comes to us with an assignment from another area we have to find a way to understand that piece of writing.

M: We look to see, does the assignment have a purpose?

H: For next time, could you bring a piece of writing that is meaningful/good/important to you, from your own area or what strikes you?

K: Maybe because I don't have a department . . . I don't think as departmentally as you guys do.

M: All these separate disciplines weren't regarded that way until the German school of the 1890s . . . Prior to that it was all conceived of holistically.

H: In modern life, we are separated by our own knowledge, in every classroom, even in the community college.

P: Everything that rises must converge. . . . [recounting a conversation with a student writing in a complex, confusing way], I asked him, "Why do you write this way? . . . What do you want to keep us out for?"

[Next Day]

H: We face a dilemma. On the one hand we each bring with [us] particular perspectives peculiar to our disciplines. On the other hand do our students [require] a less specialized knowledge? . . . Do we want to make them English majors or do we want to give them something more general?

M: I think what I'm trying to do in my course is try to give my students what it is like being a historian and not with the view that they will be historians but more with the view that there are certain things everyone should do. And that is, to be very aware of your sources, where you get information, you're very aware of the authors and their perspectives, when they were born, the social class they came from, the influences on their lives. You look at the arguments they make. Are they insightful? Do they make sense? Are the inferences that are drawn credible? That's the kind of thing that I want my students to get out of it . . . and to transfer that to other things in life. When they pick up the newspaper every morning, they realize that it is a profit-making organization and what they read may not be the whole story.

H: . . . that would have application outside of history.

M: Right.

PM: [In the field of dental hygiene, Pat wants her students to ask] Are the studies credible? Could they be repeated? These are very important observations. . . . There are a lot of untruths out there, a lot of myths. Out of the blue I can draw one: Every time a woman is pregnant she's going to lose a tooth. That's ridiculous. But it's "common knowledge." I have to dispel those myths. . . . You have to have students probe the things that they have always held to be truth. I don't care what the discipline is. Writing helps to reinforce that . . . a healthy skepticism.

H: Are there certain skills that are important to your area? Like observation?

PM: Making connections between observations. That's really important.

H: Can you be more concrete?

PM: In an oral exam, making connections [between] an observation [and what] you've read in textbooks about conditions that might apply, viral or chemical burn. Bleeding or poor gum tissue can be the result of many things. Students need to be able to look at it and put the pieces of knowledge together, the information from the patient, visually observing what they are seeing, connecting it to what they already know—integrating it.

D: I call that the "so what hypothesis?" You apply that to any statement that you read or any fact that you agree is the reality. So what if that happens? What does that mean to you as a practitioner? What does that mean to your clientele?

H: I would think that to be very important. To try to connect what they get in the class with the clinical.

PM: Where is this going to take you? What are the priorities in the situation? What are the referrals that need to be made? What are the tooth-brushing habits? or dietary habits?

K: I think that's the important thing in many of the courses, application being a higher-order thinking skill. I had a student in the writing lab who came with a piece of writing from history, a family history paper, in which she had to connect her personal history with the class material. But she had two different sections: This happened in the world. This happened in my family.

D: Do the rest of you deal in your areas with the fact that what is true today may not be true tomorrow? I do a lot of that in class. Do you have that in history, with new findings, changed perspectives?

M: Sure, . . . that's what I meant when I said when did the authors write? It plays a major role in terms of the way they view things.

H: A lot of disciplines are looking at the truth as something constructed by men and women and something that can be overturned down the road. That's how revolutions occur. You have a body of knowledge accepted by institutions and communities and someone like Galileo comes along and they have to rethink it. Knowledge is evolving, that is the subject of discussion, argument, and then consensus. We agree as a group of experts in this particular field this is what occurs, this is the truth for the moment.

M: At the moment there are multiple truths. For example, a lot of historical textbooks do not assign any role to ordinary people. It was these powerful men at the top who did everything. That was one truth. . . . Revolutions are not made by men at the top but by millions for whatever reason.

K: I think getting students to analyze problems is the most important thing. Because who knows what they will face next year or the year after?

M: . . . you leave yourselves open to new evidence. This makes sense now. And if new evidence comes along then you have to be a kind of thinker and not be dogmatic and rigid and say I can't accept this kind of evidence. Some of the paradigms have to change.

D: The problem that I see . . . is the culture lag. The student may have advanced knowledge but the public that they are working with doesn't. . . . You are really powerless because you have this information but maybe other people don't. In history it must be very frustrating if you have all this information and you're talking to a traditionalist.

H: Do students feel that history is essentially what they get in the text?

M: Or less than that. It's one story that happens.

H: Are you trying to give them something different?

M: Yes, the focus is on ordinary people, women, people of color, people who are left out of the books. So here is what history looks like from their point of view.

D: It would be a great writing assignment to have students read a traditional tack about some event in history and then give them a family structure, occupation, sex, and age, and then have them react to what is being said, what is happening to them.

M: In the critical institute I went to we were given accounts of a British soldier, another British soldier captured by the Americans, and an American soldier—all at the battle of Lexington. We looked at how they all thought—quite different.

PM: . . . I have tried to present historical introductions in my own course. Thirty years ago, dental hygiene changed dramatically. . . . When you bring it home to them, students are fascinated by history.

M: Students are very excited and challenged by the notion of not just one story.

H: Once we get students to see these multiple perspectives, we need to show them the way to ferret out the truth.

M: What they need to know is their class interests. . . . What I want my students to get out of this is . . . let me go back and look, three, four, five years prior to colonialism [in terms of Rwanda's current situation]. . . . If I take a snapshot of you now, it doesn't tell me where you've been. I think people need to have an attitude of exploration. Let me explore further. Let me not take things at face value. I wouldn't even mind if people came up with positions diametrically opposed to mine as long as they were well thought out. That they looked at the implications of what they were saying, that they really thought about it. But you don't see it.

D: That's not the reality. People base their ideas on emotions.

P: I was thinking of Hawthorne: When the American people vote with their brains, they almost always get it wrong. When they vote with their hearts, they almost always get it right.

H: You're obviously trying to get us to strike a balance here between the idea that students need to be more critical, perhaps even more intellectual, and what you are talking about, more emotion, more heart.

P: And intuition.

H: For some of us, Peter is interjecting an idea that may be alien to us, depending on our disciplines. I know that in some disciplines, the use of the "I," the intrusion of the observer, is risky, whereas Peter and I, or others around the table, may be more comfortable reading student writing or more professional material that is more personal. I notice that all of us are trying to get at the common ground, the things that all of us have in common. It's not surprising, given the institution, given our own backgrounds.

[A colleague who teaches chemistry] was talking about an assignment in which he asks students to report on all the things they see when observing a candle burning. And students came up with about fifty different details of that image. Actually the assignment was even more complex than that. First of all students were to write down what happens when a candle burns, then light the candle and observe in as much detail as they could what they saw. What is it that he is asking his students to do? And is what he is asking his students to do different from what we would ask our students to do in our own areas?

J: . . . testing the things they thought they knew. Then they are learning new things by going through the process. That's an extremely important concept. That's essentially what we're all doing here anyway. Trying to get people to explore and to test their beliefs. To seek the truth, maybe.

D: I would see it differently. In my field what I find is that observation skills can be developed. You can train yourself to be more observant. You do it in psychology, right . . . by having certain guidelines that you use.

CG: You need terms. You need to know what you're looking for. In fact if you don't have terms or concepts you're blind. So in chemistry you're always asking, what's the unit of analysis? What are the basis elements that are a way of understanding? I think it's the same in psychology except there are several different units. For instance, when the person comes into a room a Freudian would describe that person much differently than would a behaviorist. There are certain categories or terms with which the observation is made. And likewise in chemistry, things like temperature, the rate a candle is burning.

D: So depending on the field you can develop the skills. In this group we would be coming with a different frame of reference for what we would be looking for in the burning of the candle. But you can develop the skills you need for your particular area. An artist would describe it in a totally different way than a scientist.

K: The task was to make students keener observers. I certainly wouldn't have seen fifty things, but the experience would have opened my eyes to see the next reality, I hope, from another perspective.

D: But you would have to have a frame of reference as to why you're looking at the candle.

H: I think we would agree that observation is key to all our areas.

M: In that article when they talk about teaching students to see patterns—that's what we try to do in history. That's one of my goals, to get them to see patterns. Usually history is taught about discrete events.

J: Same with me. . . .

H: The pattern of a word problem, the pattern of a short story or a poem. This may be a term that cuts across the disciplines. Or you may be looking through a particular concept or category, as Chris was saying. I guess what we're saying is that [our colleague in chemistry] is looking for many of the things that we are. However, Chris used the term disciplinary focus—it may be a matter of emphasis. Observation may be more important for his students to have—to see fifty details, if that is the case, in a burning candle. Is it a matter of focus or even more profound?

CG: In terms of all the disciplines, there are boundaries. There's overlap but there are boundaries. For example, physics differs from chemistry—rules . . . collide—and biology differs from chemistry . . . .That's one of the keys when students begin to pick up on the boundaries and recognizing the boundaries. And bring that to bear in the class.

M: Is it boundaries or conventions?

P: Or metaphor?

M: There's a tendency to say one or the other. But it's probably both.

D: . . . sometimes students are given assignments without knowing the value or purpose of the assignment. Sometimes it's almost as if we are afraid of giving away the secret.

M: I'm afraid I'm going to give away the assignment. I'm nowhere explicit enough and I assume all kinds of things.

CG: What do you mean giving away the assignment?

M: For example, the Renaissance. I think "Renaissance" has a much broader meaning today than it actually did, when it referred to a literary movement. When we think of Renaissance, it can refer to a lot of things. One of the things I try to have them do is define Renaissance. I give them lots of sources.

K: Chris's question was, What were you afraid to tell them?

M: Students will ask, "What do you mean, 'define Renaissance'?" Well, was it the same for the peasants as it was for the elite? The more I talk the more I elaborate but I am also letting out the choices for them.

H: We want to give the model, the structure, the help, but there are times also when we want to hang back and let them struggle with ideas.

D: . . . but if you have a concept of where you want them to arrive then I think you owe them . . .

M: I don't have a concept of where I want them to arrive.

CG: I agree with Diane. I think you did, from what you were just saying. What you wanted them to do was bring class analysis to answer that question. An economic analysis of the question of the Renaissance. That's actually one of your categories. One of the lenses through which you want your students to see history. And laying that out to them—they're still going to have to struggle to analyze—but the term might guide them, might be a way to handle it.

Works Cited

Albert, Janice M. 1994. "I Am Not the Look in Your Eyes." In Mark Reynolds, ed. *Two-Year College English: Essays for a New Century*. Urbana, IL: National Council of Teachers of English. 9–15.

Angelo, Thomas A., and K. Patricia Cross. 1993. *Classroom Assessment Techniques: A Handbook for College Teachers*. San Francisco: Jossey-Bass.

Bakhtin, Mikhail. 1981. *The Dialogic Imagination: Four Essays*. Trans. Caryl Emerson and Michael Holquist. Ed. Michael Holquist. Austin: University of Texas Press.

Bartholomae, David. 1986. "Inventing the University." *Journal of Basic Writing* 5:4–23.

———. 1993. "The Tidy House: Basic Writing in the American Curriculum." *Journal of Basic Writing* 12:4–21.

Bazerman, Charles. 1988. *Shaping Written Knowledge: The Genre and Activity of the Experimental Article in Science*. Madison: University of Wisconsin Press.

Behar, Ruth. 1993. *Translated Woman: Crossing the Border with Esperanza's Story*. Boston: Beacon.

Berthoff, Ann E. 1978. *Forming, Thinking, Writing: The Composing Imagination*. Rochelle Park, NJ: Hayden.

———. 1987. "Dialectical Notebooks and the Audit of Meaning." In Toby Fulwiler, ed., *The Journal Book*. Portsmouth, NH: Boynton/Cook. 11–18.

Boyer, Ernest L. *Scholarship Reconsidered: Priorities of the Professoriate*. 1990. Princeton: Carnegie Foundation for the Advancement of Teaching.

Brannon, Lil, and C. H. Knoblauch. 1984. *Rhetorical Traditions and the Teaching of Writing*. Upper Montclair, NJ: Boynton/Cook.

Bruffee, Kenneth A. 1984. "Collaborative Learning and the 'Conversation of Mankind.'" *College English* 46:635–52.

———. 1993. *Collaborative Learning: Higher Education, Interdependence, and the Authority of Knowledge*. Baltimore: Johns Hopkins University Press.

———. 1993. Keynote Speech. Tenth Anniversary of Peer Tutoring, Brown University.

Bruner, Jerome. 1990. *Acts of Meaning*. Cambridge: Harvard University Press.

Building Communities: A Vision for a New Century. 1988. Washington, DC: American Association of Community and Junior Colleges, National Center for Higher Education.

Calkins, Lucy M. 1985. "Forming Research Communities among Naturalistic Researchers." In Ben W. McClelland and Timothy R. Donovan, eds. *Perspectives on Research and Scholarship in Composition*. New York: Modern Language Association. 125–44.

Clifford, James. 1986. "Introduction: Partial Truths." In James Clifford and George E. Marcus, eds. *Writing Culture: The Poetics and Politics of Ethnography*. Berkeley: University of California Press. 1–26.

Cohen, Arthur M., and Florence B. Brawer. 1982. *The American Community College*. San Francisco: Jossey-Bass.

Daiker, Donald, and Max Morenberg. 1990. *The Writing Teacher as Researcher: Essays in the Theory and Practice of Class-Based Research.* Portsmouth, NH: Boynton/Cook.

Elbow, Peter. 1973. *Writing without Teachers.* London and New York: Oxford University Press.

———. 1981. *Writing with Power: Techniques for Mastering the Writing Process.* New York: Oxford University Press.

———. 1986. *Embracing Contraries: Explorations in Learning and Teaching.* New York: Oxford University Press.

Elbow, Peter, and Jennifer Clarke. 1987. "Desert Island Discourse: The Benefits of Ignoring Audience." In Toby Fulwiler, ed. *The Journal Book.* London: Heinemann. 19–32.

Faigley, Lester. 1992. *Fragments of Rationality: Postmodernity and the Subject of Composition.* Pittsburgh: University of Pittsburgh Press.

Freire, Paulo, and Donaldo Macedo. 1987. *Literacy: Reading the Word and the World.* South Hadley, MA: Bergin and Garvey.

Fulwiler, Toby. 1987. "Introduction." In Toby Fulwiler, ed. *The Journal Book.* Portsmouth, NH: Boynton/Cook. 1–8.

Geertz, Clifford. 1983. *Local Knowledge: Further Essays in Interpretive Anthropology.* New York: Basic.

———. 1995. *After the Fact: Two Countries, Four Decades, One Anthropologist.* Cambridge: Harvard University Press.

Giroux, Henry. 1992. *Border Crossings: Cultural Workers and the Politics of Education.* New York: Routledge.

Goswami, Dixie, and Peter Stillman, eds. 1987. *Reclaiming the Classroom: Teacher Research as an Agency for Change.* Upper Montclair, NJ: Boynton/Cook.

Kadar, Andrew G. 1994. "The Sex-Bias Myth in Medicine." *Atlantic Monthly* 274 (August): 66–70.

Kantor, Kenneth J., Dan R. Kirby, and Judith P. Goetz. 1981. "Research in Context: Ethnographic Studies in English Education." *Research in the Teaching of English* 15:293–309.

Kaplan, Robert B. 1966. "Cultural Thought Patterns in Inter-Cultural Education." *Language Learning: A Journal of Applied Linguistics* 16:1–20.

Kestel, Fran. 1994. "Are You up to Date on Diabetes Medication?" *American Journal of Nursing* (July): 48–52.

Kuhn, Thomas. *The Structure of Scientific Revolutions.* 1962. Chicago: University of Chicago Press.

Langer, Judith A. 1992. "Speaking of Knowing: Conceptions of Understanding in Academic Disciplines." In Ann Herrington and Charles Moran, eds. *Writing, Teaching, and Learning in the Disciplines.* New York: Modern Language Association. 69–85.

LeBlond, C. Merry. 1992. "The Student Journal: Its Use in Teaching Ethics in Dental Hygiene Programs." *Education Update* 12:11–13.

London, Howard. 1978. *The Culture of a Community College.* New York: Praeger.

Lu, Min-Zhan. 1991. "Redefining the Legacy of Mina Shaughnessy: A Critique of the Politics of Linguistic Innocence." *Journal of Basic Writing* 10:26–40.

————. 1992. "Conflict and Struggle: The Enemies or Preconditions of Basic Writing?" *College English* 54:887–913.

Macrorie, Ken. 1970. *Uptaught.* New York: Hayden.

McGrath, Dennis, and Martin B. Spear. 1991. *The Academic Crisis of the Community College.* Albany: State University of New York Press.

Meyer, Emily, and Louise Z. Smith. 1987. *The Practical Tutor.* New York: Oxford University Press.

Nelson, Sandra J., and Laura MacLeod. 1993. "The Analytical Report: Development of Cases for Business Report Writing Classes." *Business Education Forum* 48:36–38.

North, Stephen M. 1984. "The Idea of a Writing Center." *College English* 46:433–46.

Odell, Lee. 1992. "Context-Specific Ways of Knowing and the Evaluation of Writing." In Ann Herrington and Charles Moran, eds. *Writing, Teaching, and Learning in the Disciplines.* New York: Modern Language Association. 86–98.

Ong, Walter J. 1982. *Orality and Literacy: The Technologizing of the Word.* London and New York: Methuen.

Pratt, Mary Louise. 1986. "Fieldwork in Common Places." In James Clifford and George E. Marcus, eds. *Writing Culture: The Poetics and Politics of Ethnography.* Berkeley: University of California Press. 27–50.

————. 1992. *Imperial Eyes: Travel Writing and Transculturation.* London and New York: Routledge.

Raines, Helon Howell. 1994. "Tutoring and Teaching: Continuum, Dichotomy, or Dialectic?" *The Writing Center Journal* 14:150–62.

Ray, Ruth E. 1993. *The Practice of Theory: Teacher Research in Composition.* Urbana, IL: National Council of Teachers of English.

Rorty, Richard. 1979. *Philosophy and the Mirror of Nature.* Princeton: Princeton University Press.

Rosaldo, Renato. 1993. *Culture and Truth: The Remaking of Social Analysis.* 2d ed. Boston: Beacon.

Shaughnessy, Mina P. 1977. *Errors and Expectations: A Guide for the Teacher of Basic Writing.* New York: Oxford University Press.

Smoke, Trudy. 1992. *A Writer's Workbook: An Interactive Writing Text for ESL Students.* 2d ed. New York: St. Martin's.

Sommers, Nancy. 1982. "Responding to Student Writers." *College Composition and Communication* 33:148–57.

Stavrianos, L. S. 1992. *Lifelines from Our Past: A New World History.* Armonk, NY: M. E. Sharpe.

Tinberg, Howard B. 1993. "Border-Crossings: Shaping the Academic Conversation." *Advanced Composition Forum* 5:8–11.

————. 1993. "Seeing Ourselves Differently: Remaking Research and Scholarship at the Community College." *Teaching English in the Two-Year College* 20:12–17.

Vaughan, George B. 1994. "Scholarship and Teaching: Crafting the Art." In Mark Reynolds, ed. *Two-Year College English: Essays for a New Century.* Urbana, IL: National Council of Teachers of English. 212–21.

Walvoord, Barbara E., and Lucile McCarthy. 1990. *Thinking and Writing in College: A Naturalistic Study of Students in Four Disciplines.* Urbana, IL: National Council of Teachers of English.

West, Cornel. 1989. *The American Evasion of Philosophy: A Genealogy of Pragmatism.* Madison: University of Wisconsin Press.

Index

91

Author

Howard B. Tinberg teaches in the English department at Bristol Community College, where he also directs the college's writing lab. His publications have appeared in a variety of journals, including *College Composition and Communication, College English,* and *Teaching English in the Two-Year College.* He also currently serves on the College Section Steering Committee of the National Council of Teachers of English.

This book was typeset in Baskerville by Electronic Imaging, Inc.
Typefaces used on the cover were Erazure, Mantinia, and Electra.
The book was printed on Offset 70 lb. paper, by Versa Press, Inc.